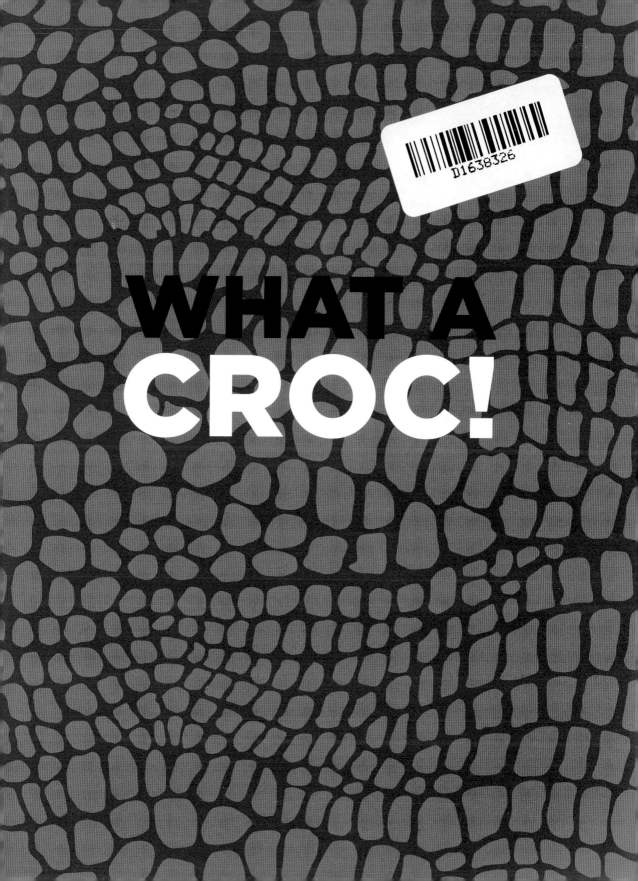

WHAT A
CROC!

WHAT A CROC!

LEGENDARY FRONT PAGES FROM THE
NT News

hachette
AUSTRALIA

hachette
AUSTRALIA

Published in Australia and New Zealand in 2014
by Hachette Australia
(an imprint of Hachette Australia Pty Limited)
Level 17, 207 Kent Street, Sydney NSW 2000
www.hachette.com.au

10 9 8 7 6 5

A catalogue record for this book is available from the National Library of Australia.

ISBN 978 0 7336 3352 2

Cover and internal design by Christabella Designs
Typesetting and internal layout by Isabel Staas
Colour reproduction by Splitting Image, Melbourne
Printed in China by 1010 Printing

Hachette Australia's policy is to use papers that are natural, renewable and recyclable products and made from wood grown in sustainable forests. The logging and manufacturing processes are expected to conform to the environmental regulations of the country of origin.

CONTENTS

INTRODUCTION

POPULATION-WISE, Darwin and the Northern Territory are quite small in the grand scheme of things.

And so is the daily paper that serves them.

The entire NT population is about one-third of that of an average Sydney suburb, and the annual budget of the editorial workforce of the *NT News* – the Territory's main newspaper since 1952 – would probably be smaller* than the personal sports betting accounts of most other capital city editors. (*Based on no research whatsoever.)

But ask just about anyone – no matter where they're from – if they've heard of the *NT News* and the answer will be a yes . . . and probably a chuckle.

The *NT News* has become the little paper that could.

Although most seem to think it has always relied on being quirky to push sales and build its brand, it only really started consistently running, ahem, 'different' front pages for the past half-decade or so, despite being around for over 60 years.

There was a moment in time when the editorial team decided that whatever the most talked-about story of the day in the newsroom was, it should be on the front page because logic dictated it would be the most talked-about story of the day outside the office too. And that meant tales of nude bank robbers or talking cats were, from then on, always going to beat out stories about politicians or tax reform for the prime spot on the front page.

It wasn't long before those front pages began to take on a life of their own outside of the Territory. It wasn't unusual for *NT News* journos to be sent images of their own front pages from friends in France . . . or Fiji . . . or Finland . . . with the message, 'Check this crazy paper out. You guys should start doing front pages like this!' Yeah, thanks.

Suddenly, the little *NT News* had become many people's second favourite newspaper (after their own home-town paper).

Territorians now often refer to the *NT News* as the paper that relies on the 3 Cs – crocs, cyclones and crime (of the bungling crook variety). But, in truth, it is the paper of the multiple Cs – crocs, cyclones, crime, cursing cats, creatures from outer space (aliens and UFOs), cane toads, crazy critters (promiscuous pigs, dogs that think they are chickens and killer peacocks), more cane toads, and copulating couples in public. And that's just the tip of the iceberg.

NT News headline writers are encouraged to have fun, to push the envelope a little bit further than they might get away with elsewhere, and reporters and photographers are expected to search out the unusual.

The *NT News* thinks it gets its front page mix right most of the time. Hopefully others agree.

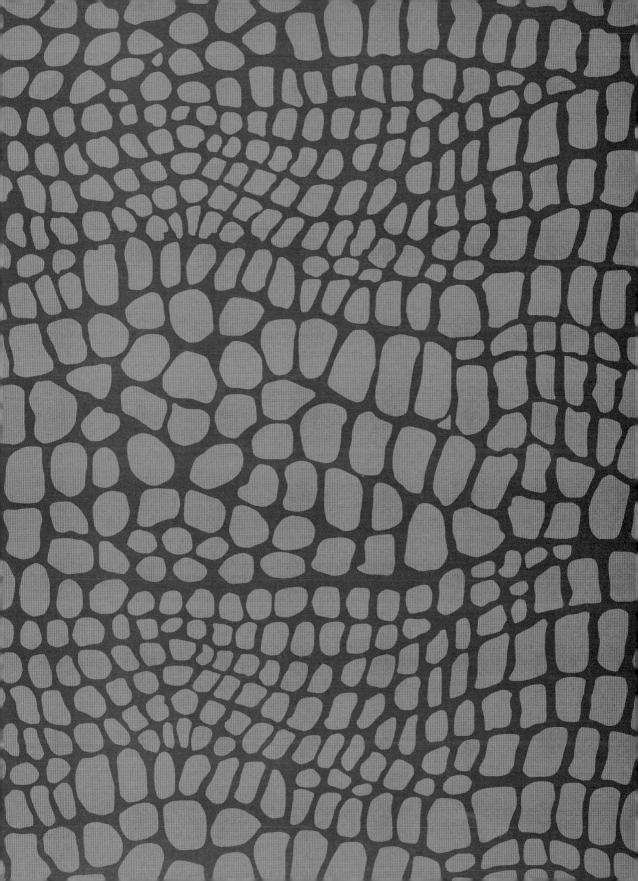

CROCS V WORLD

THERE are more crocs in the NT than there are people in its capital city of Darwin. So it makes sense that they would feature on the *NT News*' front pages more often than people do.

And even though Top Enders spend an inordinate amount of their time explaining to others that we don't share our streets with giant man-eating salties, they do tend to turn up in a lot of unexpected places. Like backyard swimming pools, pubs, buses, playgrounds, workshops and, yes, sometimes on our streets.

The second most overheard phrase in the NT after: 'It's hot!' is 'Where would the *NT News* be without its crocs?' What can we say, except . . . 'True dat!'

NT❂News

YOUR VOICE IN THE TERRITORY

News Destination PANPA **2011** AWARDS Of The Year

Tuesday, November 15, 2011   ntnews.com.au $1.20 Country freight 20 cents extra Incl GST

WIN A TRIP TO THE AUSTRALIAN OPEN
DETAILS ≫P36

AXE ATTACK IN VICIOUS STREET BRAWL
STORY ≫P3

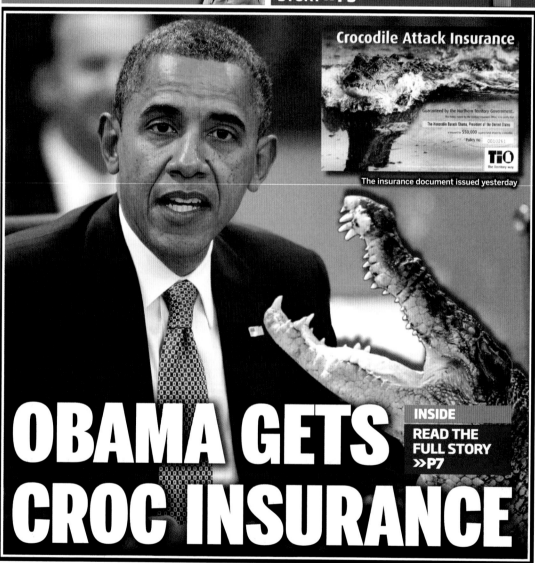

Crocodile Attack Insurance

Guaranteed by the Northern Territory Government.

The Honorable Barack Obama, President of the United States

is insured to $50,000 against total attack by a crocodile

*Policy no.   OO10261

TiO
the Territory way

The insurance document issued yesterday

OBAMA GETS CROC INSURANCE

INSIDE
READ THE FULL STORY
≫P7

MAUBOY IN MID-AIR DRAMA AS SHE FLIES HOME TO PLAY FOR PRESIDENT ⟩ P3

TOT BEACH PARTY 2NITE @ HP!

NT ♦ News

YOUR VOICE IN THE TERRITORY

Thursday, August 5, 2010   ntnews.com.au $1.20 Country freight 20 cents extra Incl GST

AS BIG AS A TRUCK

Two LandCruisers needed to pull cattle-killing saltie out of river

INSIDE ▸ Story P2

GREENS WANT TO BAN FISHING » P2

TEETH BLING
NT's latest fashion fad » P3

LINGERIE MODEL COMP DISCOVERY SAT NITE

NT News

YOUR VOICE IN THE TERRITORY

Tuesday, July 12, 2011 · ntnews.com.au · $1.20 *Country price $2.00* Incl GST

2010 PANPA Newspaper of The Year Awards

YES, IT'S REAL

NT NEWS photographer Katrina Bridgeford took this amazing photograph of Brutus, a 5.5m saltwater croc, giving a boatload of tourists a moment they'll never forget on the Adelaide River last week.

FULL STORY ❯ P2

GILLARD AND ABBOTT ARE LIARS, NT COURT HEARS ❯ P3

HOOPERS T.O.T. BEACH PARTY LOST ARC TONIGHT

NORTHERN TERRITORY NEWS

Phone: 8944 9900 CLASSIFIEDS: 8944 9999   DARWIN: Saturday, July 8, 2006 $1.60* (Country Freight 30 cents extra) Incl. GST

Is this the biggest croc ever seen in NT

WHAT A CROC: The giant saltie (TOP) photographed at Corroboree by Ted Jackson and (ABOVE) *NT News* photographer Peter Bennett's famous picture of Sweetheart

By REBEKAH CAVANAGH

A GIANT saltwater crocodile at least 6m long and 1m wide has been photographed at a popular Territory fishing spot.

The monster — estimated at more than 6.5m long — has been basking on the banks of the Mary River at Corroboree Billabong, about 90km east of Darwin.

The Territory's most famous croc, Sweetheart, measured 5.1m. The two largest certifiably measured

Continued Page 5

'Sweetheart' 5.1m

'Corroboree croc' 6.5m?

YOUR VOICE IN THE TERRITORY

NT News

Wednesday, August 6, 2014   ntnews.com.au $1.20   Country freight 20 cents extra   Incl GST

Picture:
ANDREW PAICE

GREAT
AUSTRALIAN
BITE

Jaws v Claws

Brutus, the 5.5m croc, wins titanic battle with big bull shark P2

YOUR VOICE IN THE TERRITORY

NT★News

Tuesday, July 2, 2013　　　ntnews.com.au　　　**$1.20** Country freight 20 cents extra Incl GST

DOG ATTACKED WITH STANLEY KNIFE
REPORT ≫P3

THE NIGHT THE NT GOES CRACKERS
TERRITORY DAY ≫P6-7

Video online
nt**news**.com.au

ES, IT'S REAL
FULL STORY ≫P2

BRUTUS GOES THE WHOLE HOG

Brutus shot to international fame when he featured on the NT News front page in July 2011

INSIDE

FULL STORY ≫P2

TOURISTS WATCH IN SHOCK AS CROC SHOWS THEM WHO'S THE BOSS

NT☆News

YOUR VOICE IN THE TERRITORY

Friday, October 28, 2011   ntnews.com.au $1.20 Country freight 30 cents extra Incl GST

MISS OUT ON YOUR ESSENTIAL 40-PAGE CYCLONE SURVIVAL GUIDE YESTERDAY?

FIND OUT HOW TO GET YOUR COPY ≫P2

CYCLONE

It's enough to make you ship yourself

REPORT ▶ P3

Picture: ROBBY SHERRY

NAKED DRIVER CAUGHT ON VIDEO

INSIDE
FULL
STORY
≫P2

POLLIES AT WAR OVER SEX GESTURE ▶ P5

NT✦News

YOUR VOICE IN THE TERRITORY

Thursay, July 22, 2010

ntnews.com.au

$1.20 Country freight 20 cents extra Incl GST

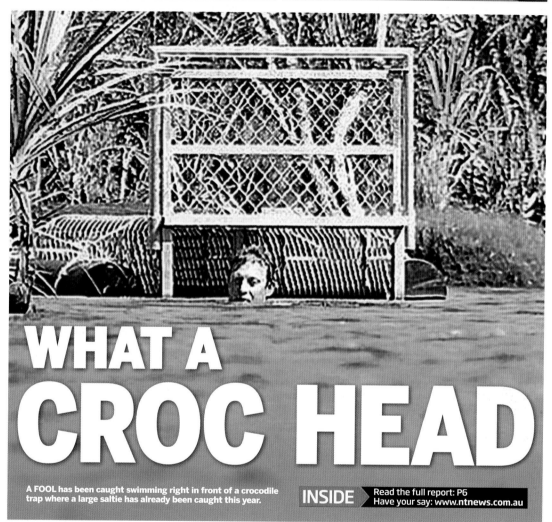

WHAT A CROC HEAD

A FOOL has been caught swimming right in front of a crocodile trap where a large saltie has already been caught this year.

INSIDE Read the full report: P6
Have your say: www.ntnews.com.au

FATMAN SCOOP LIVE DISCOVERY SUN 25 JULY

NT☆News

YOUR VOICE IN THE TERRITORY

Saturday, June 11, 2011 — ntnews.com.au — $1.60 Country freight 30cents extra Incl GST

WHAT A PLANKER

INSIDE
READ THE FULL STORY >>P10

WOMAN PHOTOGRAPHED LYING ON 4.65m, 600kg CROC

HALF-TONNE CROC ATTACKS BOAT
>> FULL STORY P10

BAREFOOT BOWLS NIGHTCLIFF SPORTS CLUB @ 5.30PM

YOUR VOICE IN THE TERRITORY

NT News

Monday, November 18, 2013   ntnews.com.au $1.20 Country freight 20 cents extra Incl GST

2012 BRAND OF THE YEAR

COULD THIS BE OUR WETTEST NOVEMBER EVER?

STORY » P5

REVEALED: WHY YOU'RE PAYING TOO MUCH FOR YOUR AIRFARES

REPORT » P9

YEP, IT'S A TERRITORY ROAD BLOCK

STORY P4

PLUS AMAZING PICTURES: CROC TAKES ON ELEPHANT >> P3

DUMB AND DUMBER

WOMAN, 29, CAUGHT DRUNK AT THE WHEEL TWICE ... ON THE SAME NIGHT ... IN THE SAME CAR ... IN THE SAME SPOT >> P4

NORTHERN TERRITORY NEWS

Arafura Games
The official newspaper
of the Arafura Games

Phone: 8944 9900 Classifieds: 8944 9999 www.ntnews.com.au

Wednesday, May 13, 2009

$1.20* (Country freight 20 cents extra) Incl. GST

A croc walks into a bar
NO, SERIOUSLY

By NADJA HAINKE

A TERRITORY croc sought the safety of a bar after it was caught lurking on a verandah in Darwin's rural area.

Witness Peter Donovan said the bar visitor was a "unique Territory

Continued Page 2

THE SQUEEZE IS ON – AND WE'RE NOT TALKING ABOUT THE BUDGET

A STUNNED group of Territory dinner party guests watched on as this huge python dropped in on them with an adult possum in its grip then proceeded to swallow it in front of them STORY › P3

READER PIC

BUDGET '09
Coverage: P4,5,6,7

HEALTH	DEFENCE	INDIGENOUS	NT PROJECTS
$28million for a new medical school in Darwin	$160million upgrades to Defence bases	$807million to continue the Intervention	$50million to upgrade the Port of Darwin
$34million to set up a Centre of Excellence in Indigenous Health and Education	$38.5million for an early warning aircraft facility	$50million to build "a more efficient native title system"	$2million to upgrade roads in Darwin, Palmerston and Litchfield
$13.6million to Alice Springs Hospital Emergency Department	A new Cyber Security Operations Centre to monitor cyber threats	$204million for remote primary health care, eye and ear health, dental care and pathology services	$1million to fix blackspots
	New artillery, light vehicles and improved small-arms for army		

New teaching hospitals for NT

THE Territory will have its own home-grown doctors for the first time after last night's Federal Budget.

Two medical teaching hospitals will be built to allow Territorians to study all four years of medicine in Darwin. The NT is currently only capable of training medical students in their last two years.

These two new teaching facilities will be at Royal Darwin Hospital and Charles Darwin University.

Construction is expected to start next financial year, with the first intake of students in 2011.

The Budget also included $18.6 million to build an accommodation complex of 50 units at Royal Darwin Hospital for patients and carers.

FULL STORY: P5

MINISTRY OF SOUND DISCOVERY THIS SAT

NT News

YOUR VOICE IN THE TERRITORY

Tuesday, September 11, 2012 ntnews.com.au $1.20 Country freight 20 cents extra Incl GST

JOIN OUR CAMPAIGN TO HELP SAVE LIVES
SPEAK UP » P4

AFL PLAYER DIES IN LAS VEGAS
FOOTY WORLD IN SHOCK » P3

Dean Bennett, Matt Davis and John "Snapper" Curwen-Walker were asleep in their boat on the South Alligator River when it was attacked by a croc

Picture: ELISE DERWIN

CROC EATS BOAT

Fishos' terrifying encounter with rogue saltie REVEALED P2

YOUR VOICE IN THE TERRITORY

NT★News

PANPA 2011 AWARDS — News Destination Of The Year

Wednesday, August 8, 2012   ntnews.com.au $1.20 Country freight 20cents extra Incl GST

ALL THE FASHIONS, FILLIES AND FELLAS FROM THE CUP

OUT AND ABOUT ≫P17

DARWIN FESTIVAL IN RACISM STORM

REPORT ≫P3

Picture: GAVIN BEDFORD

CROCKY HORROR PICTURE SHOW

INSIDE FULL STORY ≫P2

Idiot risks life and ... er ... manhood for snap on a trap

NORTHERN TERRITORY NEWS

Phone: 8944 9900 Classifieds: 8944 9999 www.ntnews.com.au

Thursday, November 15, 2007

$1.20* (Country freight 20 cents extra) Incl. GST

16 pages

RELOCATION NORTH

A guide for defence families new to the Top End
>>>INSIDE

First cyclone of the season forms
>>>PAGE 3

CROCODILE UNDIE

Commando croc hunter catches saltie with jocks

By **REBEKAH CAVANAGH**

A MAN has gone "commando" in an attempt to rescue a 1.5m saltwater crocodile stranded on a popular Darwin beach.

Jimmy Howard told last night how he lassoed the saltie before taking off his red jocks and putting them over its eyes to calm it down.

"I just ripped my jocks off, soaked them in the water and wrapped them around its face," the ballsy Territorian said. "It was a bit cranky and that was the only thing I could use to cover its eyes.

"I'm probably the only one in the world who can say they went commando for a croc. I'm just lucky it wasn't a bull — it would have arced up a bit at the sight of red jocks."

Mr Howard, 35, almost stepped on the croc as it basked in a shallow pool of water more than 100m from the water's edge at Casuarina Beach about 2.30pm on Monday. "I was walking along at low tide and noticed a small outline in the water and thought it was a stingray," he said.

"I was standing about a metre from its tail, so I quickly backstepped and grabbed a stick, which I then poked at it to make sure it was alive.

"It had 200m of sand all around it and was just sitting in the pool of water, which was probably only half a metre deep.

"He was only a little fella, so he probably got a bit tired in the rough tides or something. All I know is he had good little teeth on him and I think he would have taken a good chunk or two out of you if he had the chance."

Continued Page 2

JOCK-ODILE HUNTER: Jimmy Howard went commando to control this 1.5m croc he almost stepped on at Casuarina Beach. He used his jocks to cover the croc's eyes and calm it down. Picture: FIONA MORRISON

Rudd's $1bn school pitch goes hi-tech: P6

Jetstar to set up new base in Darwin: P3

NORTHERN TERRITORY NEWS MYSTERY NUMBER

BUYING THIS PAPER COULD WIN YOU THE JACKPOT!
Money Jackpots each day Monday to Friday by $10

JACKPOT **$1380**

TO WIN INSTANTLY RING 1900 966 372 and key in your lucky number. If you win, keep this paper for verification. Call costs 55c (inc. GST). Higher from mobile/pay phones - Dialect Solutions Group.

LUCKY NUMBER

It is recommended that you use a land line touch tone phone. Some mobiles, portable and pay phones may experience technical faults due to reception complications.

NT News

YOUR VOICE IN THE TERRITORY

Monday, May 19, 2014   ntnews.com.au   **$1.20** Country freight 20 cents extra Incl GST

Picture: ROD NEWMAN

CROC'S BEEF WITH BUFF

Buffy the Croc Slayer

TONY'S TERRITORY TALES
STORY » P2

NOW THAT'S A FISH!
HOOK IN » P7

V1 - NTNE01Z01MA

NORTHERN TERRITORY NEWS

48 PAGES

Phone: 8944 9900 Classifieds: 8944 9999 www.ntnews.com.au

Friday, March 12, 2010

$1.20* (Country freight 20 cents extra) Incl. GST

GRAND FINAL
The teams, the talking points
>> Game On

ST PAT'S CUP
The field, the barriers
>>P43

DON'T CROC THE BOAT

THIS is the incredible moment when a huge, and obviously very hungry, saltwater crocodile almost launched itself into the tinny of two shocked tourists in one of the Territory's most popular fishing spots

FULL STORY >>P7

Picture: TALES FROM THE TINNY (ABC)

PARTY WITH RUMOUR @ BEACHFRONT TONIGHT

NT News

YOUR VOICE IN THE TERRITORY

Thursday, April 12, 2012 · ntnews.com.au · $1.20 Country freight 30cents extra Incl GST

HOSPITAL BLAST HERO TELLS OF SAVING MATE

REVEALED »P3

TWO WINS FOR THE UNDERDOGS

WIN 1

LIZARD 1
SNAKE 0

FULL STORY **P2**

Picture: PETER BRADY

FISH EATS CROC

WIN 2 SEE THE AMAZING PICTURE, READ THE FULL STORY **P2**

NORTHERN TERRITORY NEWS

Phone: 8944 9900 Classifieds: 8944 9999 www.ntnews.com.au   **Wednesday, March 5, 2008** $1.20* (Country freight 20 cents extra) Incl. GST

SIEGE IN THE SUBURBS
Page 7

SUMMER ENDS IN DISCONTENT
Sport

WORLD PICTURE EXCLUSIVE

G'DAY, BAIT!

'The animal clearly wanted to kill me'

THIS monster crocodile came within a metre of making a meal of fisherman Novon Mashiah on a Territory river. Novon's mate Doron Aviguy was on hand to SNAP this incredible photo. **MORE PICTURES, FULL STORY: P8**

NORTHERN TERRITORY NEWS

Official newspaper
of the Arafura Games

Phone: 8944 9900 CLASSIFIEDS: 8944 9999   DARWIN: Thursday, May 17, 2007 $1.10* (Country Freight / 20 cents extra) Incl. GST

JAWS

Meet the Top End saltie who's half the croc he used to be

PICTURE EXCLUSIVE

OUCH!: On-the-spot NEWSBREAKER Norm Davis sent us this photo of a large croc that has lost its bottom jaw, probably after a battle with an even bigger saltie

By ALISON BEVEGE

A LARGE, battle-damaged croc dubbed "Jaws" has been spotted lurking in a Territory waterway.

The presumably hungry saltie, spotted basking in the sun at Corroboree Billabong by Norm Davis and his mate Steve Jenkins on Sunday, has half its lower jaw missing.

The pair were fishing at the waterhole, about 90km southeast of Darwin, when they photographed the 4m reptile.

"I just went 'Wow! How unusual is this?'," Mr Davis said.

They moved their 5m tinnie in to have a closer look but got a shock when their boat bumped another big croc under the water.

"I didn't know I could walk in mid-air but I did," he said. "I tried to climb the invisible ladder."

The croc they hit scrambled on to the bank — and Jaws dived into the water and disappeared. Mr Davis, an army repair manager, said Jaws' wounds looked fresh.

He plans to return to the spot to try to catch sight of him again.

"Heaven forbid something would happen to the poor fella — but it's a job for Parks and Wildlife to look after him.

There's no way I'm going to try to get him into a boat," he said.

Crocodylus Park owner and croc expert Grahame Webb said Jaws was in for a tough time.

"It's a pretty severe break," Mr Webb said. "He'd have trouble feeding ... he needs the two jaws

Continued Page 2

NORTHERN TERRITORY NEWS

Ph 8944 9999 www.ntnews.com.au   Saturday, November 3, 2007 $1.60* (Country freight 30 cents extra) Incl. GST

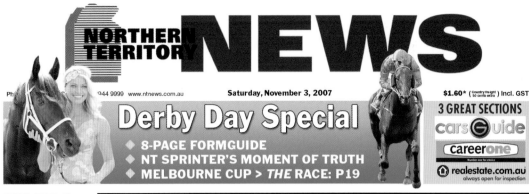

Derby Day Special

- ◆ 8-PAGE FORMGUIDE
- ◆ NT SPRINTER'S MOMENT OF TRUTH
- ◆ MELBOURNE CUP > *THE* RACE: P19

ME TOO
Howard, Rudd both in Darwin

By NICK CALACOURAS

PRIME Minister John Howard and Opposition Leader Kevin Rudd are both in Darwin today as the major parties fight for the seat of Solomon.

In an EXCLUSIVE interview with the *Northern Territory News* yesterday, the Prime Minister said he does not believe Solomon MP David Tollner is distancing himself from the Howard Government.

"I encourage all of the members to run a local campaign," he said. Mr Tollner's 2004 election campaign involved the slogan "a vote for Dave Tollner is a vote for John Howard".

But this year Mr Tollner is attacking the Territory Labor Government on law and order issues instead.

"I will say again, a vote for Dave Tollner is a vote for me," Mr Howard said.

"But that doesn't mean he shouldn't campaign locally.

"You need a duality to the campaign where you are part

Continued Page 4

JAILHOUSE CROC

Saltie spends night in prison cell

By NIGEL ADLAM

A CROCODILE has been arrested after lunging at a Territory fisherman.

The 2.75m saltie spent the night in a cell. It was taken to a crocodile farm the next morning.

Parks and Wildlife senior ranger Phil Wise said it was probably the first time a crocodile had been thrown in the slammer.

"It did its best not to be caught but wasn't aggressive — it came

From Page 2

SCALES OF JUSTICE: Sen Const Wade Marshall and Parks and Wildlife senior ranger Phil Wise with their unusual prisoner in its own cell. Pictures: NHULUNBUY POLICE

NORTHERN TERRITORY NEWS

Phone: 8944 9900 CLASSIFIEDS: 8944 9999   DARWIN: Saturday, April 29, 2006 $1.50* (Country Freight 30 cents extra) Incl. GST

Port Arthur 10 years on

Nic and Keith
set the big date

Page: 3

SATURDAY NEWS *Extra* **Pages: 13,15,16,17**

SAWTOOTH

Cranky croc steals man's chainsaw

By REBEKAH CAVANAGH

A LARGE crocodile leapt out of a pond yesterday to rip a chainsaw from a man's hands as he trimmed a tree branch metres off the ground.

Fred Buckland (*pictured below*) got the fright off his life when he was cutting a tree, which had fallen in the 4.4m saltie's pen at Corroboree Park Tavern about 10am.

Tavern owner Peter Shappert said when Cyclone Monica swept through the tourist centre — about 80km south-west of Darwin — this week, a 10m high tree fell across

Continued Page 4

NORTHERN TERRITORY NEWS

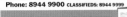

Phone: 8944 9900 CLASSIFIEDS: 8944 9999   DARWIN: Thursday, February 9, 2006 $1.10* (Country Freight 20 cents extra) Incl. GST

Crocs feast on 'DUMB' southern cows

BY GREG McLEAN

"DUMB" cows from "down south" are being *snapped up* by cunning Top End crocodiles.

Cattle from southern areas used to grazing on the good stuff next to Top End rivers are considered easy *prey* for hungry salties, who can stuff a half-tonne beast in their mouths in a fraction of a second.

Darwin angler Annette Lear captured this amazing photograph of a 5m-plus saltie dining out on a beef burger at Hardies Lagoon off the Arnhem Highway.

Continued Page 2

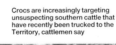

Crocs are increasingly targeting unsuspecting southern cattle that have recently been trucked to the Territory, cattlemen say

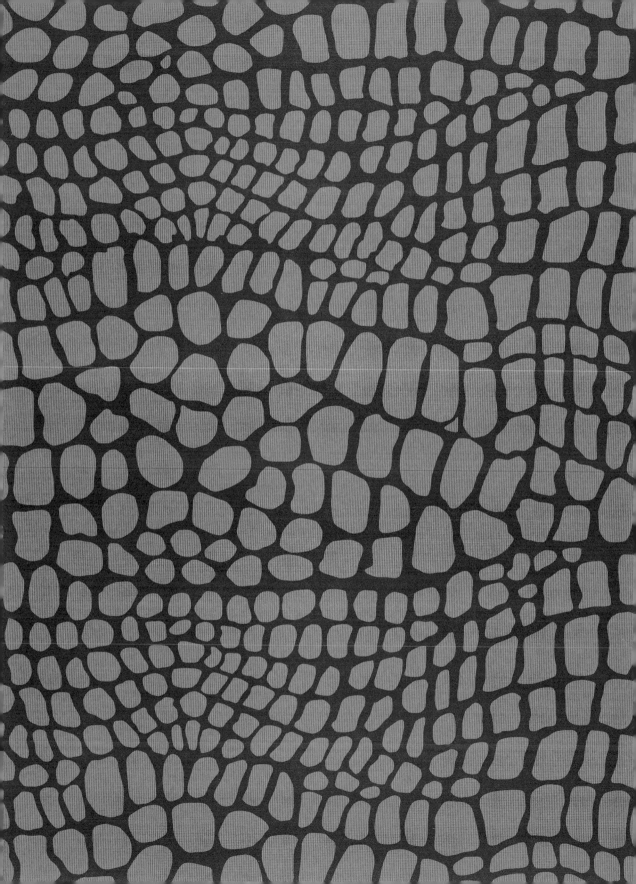

BOYS WILL
BE BOYS

THERE are lots of things for blokes to do in the Territory like fishing, drinking, hunting, drinking, mining, drinking, building things, drinking, getting nude in the middle of town and running around, drinking . . .

It's no wonder the place has the highest ratio of men to women compared to anywhere else in Australia.

It's no wonder, too, that with so many blokes knocking about together all of the time, they can find themselves in some pretty interesting situations.

It's a fair bet that the starting point for a lot of our front pages was a guy making a comment something like: 'Hey, hold my beer and watch this!'

Ah, yes, blokes. It's lucky that we have them around to help fill that big white hole on the front page. On the other hand, it's also pretty lucky that many of the women here are doctors.

NT News

YOUR VOICE IN THE TERRITORY

Tuesday, July 31, 2012 ntnews.com.au $1.20 Country freight 20 cents extra Incl GST

JOEL CARROLL'S GOLDEN DREAM BEGINS

OLYMPICS COVERAGE >> SPORT

MURDOCH MOVED TO DARWIN JAIL

FIND OUT WHY >> P3

Alex Bowden is recovering at Royal Darwin Hospital after suffering burns to his buttocks from a firecracker

WHY I STUCK A CRACKER UP MY CLACKER

VICTIM REVEALS ALL ▶ P2

NT News

YOUR VOICE IN THE TERRITORY

Saturday, February 12, 2011   ntnews.com.au $1.60 Country freight 30 cents extra Incl GST

PANPA 2010 AWARDS Newspaper of The Year

Former NT footballer murdered

REPORT ≫P9

WEDDING DRAMA

Best Man left bleeding after being hit in head by flying dildo

... and wait until you hear where it came from

Donged! ... Jure Skumavc

INSIDE   FULL STORY ≫P8

HOT 100 SINGLES PARTY @ BEACHFRONT TONIGHT!

NORTHERN TERRITORY NEWS

Phone: 8944 9900 CLASSIFIEDS: 8944 9999   **DARWIN: Wednesday, January 18, 2006** $1.10* (Country Freight 20 cents extra) Incl. GST

puzzle book #1   puzzle book #2   puzzle book #3   puzzle book #4

PULL THEM OUT, FOLD THEM, CUT THEM, SOLVE THEM!

GET YOUR SECOND PUZZLE PULL-OUT

GEE WHIZ! Vandals break into council compound to relieve themselves into parking inspectors' helmets

Leaky louts strike in wee hours

By ERIC TLOZEK
Council Reporter

VANDALS have broken into Darwin City Council headquarters and urinated in the motorcycle helmets of its parking inspectors.

The council's director of community services John Banks said yesterday: "The officers are sometimes subjected to some abuse and criticism but they shouldn't have to put up with this sort of thing," he said.

Continued: Page 2

Continued: Page 2

A Darwin parking inspector straps on his helmet yesterday. Picture: BRAD FLEET

NORTHERN TERRITORY NEWS

Phone: 8944 9900   Classifieds: 8944 9999 www.ntnews.com.au   **Wednesday, May 14, 2008** $1.20* (Country freight 20 cents extra) Incl. GST

Part 5 today
Historic croc photos

WIN

a Katherine adventure
Details, coupon: P15

Seatbelt for slab of VB, 5-year-old left unrestrained

Driver straps in beer, not boy

By TARA RAVENS

TERRITORY police were shocked when they pulled over a driver who had put a seatbelt around his slab of beer — but left a five-year-old boy unrestrained.

The child was sitting on the console between the

Continued Page 2

Picture: BARRY NATTRASS

Fire destroys part of Territory history: Story P2

BUDGET '08
Coverage: P4,5,6,7

TAXES	TERRITORIANS	EDUCATION	HEALTH	INDIGENOUS	BUSINESS	DEFENCE	ENVIRONMENT
Income tax cuts totalling $47billion over four years. Tax cuts worth $20 a week for someone on $48,000 a year. Medicare levy surcharge threshold increased.	$2.5million over five years to get NT Aussie Rules football team into southern competition. $8million for setting up Office of Northern Australia in Darwin.	$99million for extra teachers in NT over five years. 6.5 per cent increase in funding for Territory schools. $1million per NT school for computers.	Money for Palmerston super clinic. $10million for NT remote health. Share of $10billion hospital fund $600million to cut elective surgery waiting list.	$666million more for NT indigenous communities, including $154million for education, $168million for employment and $328million for intervention.	Raft of fringe benefit tax concessions removed. Tax offset rules tightened. Review of tax regime. Luxury car tax increased from 25 per cent to 33 per cent.	Defence budget $22.7billion. $42.7million to improve NT bases, 300 per cent rise. Free dental and medical care for Defence families in Katherine.	Share of $2.3billion over five years to cut greenhouse gas emissions; $500million over eight years for clean coal; $300million green loans program

---

SHORRY OFFISHER

Why am I over the limit? Coz I drank 90 cans of beer ≫ P2

8-PAGE CAULFIELD CUP RACE GUIDE | WIN A TRIP TO FIJI ≫ P23

NORTHERN TERRITORY NEWS

Phone: 8944 9900 CLASSIFIEDS: 8944 9999 DARWIN: Saturday, January 14, 2006 $1.50* (Country Freight 30 cents extra) Incl. GST

Stone the crows!
Rolf's coming to town — Page 3

Brave Kylie wins fight — Page 3

This is what *ONE* man drank in *ONE* night

... is it any wonder he fell off his bike

By REBECCA HEWETT
Court Reporter

A MAN drank 24 stubbies of beer, 12 mixed spirit cans, a bottle of Jim Beam and a cask of port — and then fell off his pushbike.

Stuart Lee Martin, 28, suffered facial

Continued: Page 2

SUNDAY Territorian

May 25, 2014 | $1.30 Country freight 20c extra. Includes GST

"I GOT SOOOO TRASHED LAST NIGHT"

Full story >> P4

A 30-year-old man, who had been sleeping in a dumpster, ended up in the back of a rubbish truck. Emergency services came to his rescue after a driver heard noises coming from the back of the truck

TOTALLY ADDICTED TO BASS
FULL WRAP-UP >> P8,9

"TAKE THE HOUSE – IT'S YOURS"
STORY >> P5

V1 - NTNE01Z01MA

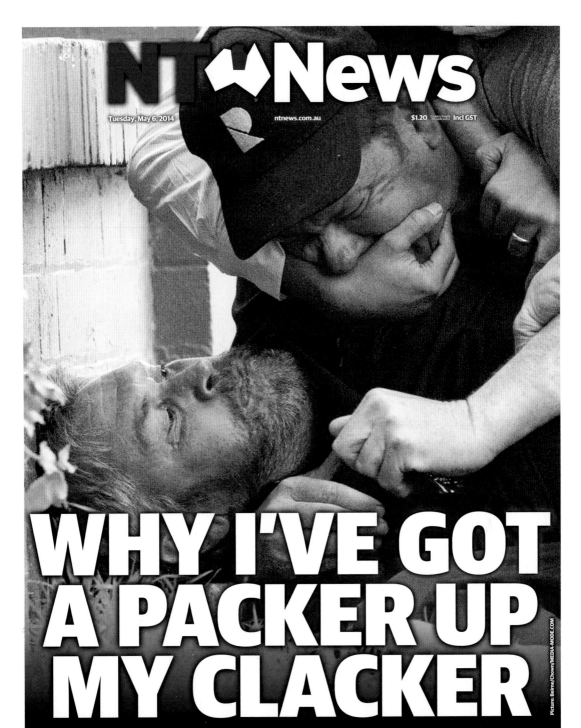

NT News

Tuesday, May 6, 2014　　ntnews.com.au　　$1.20 Country freight 70 cents extra　Incl GST

Picture: Beirne/Crown/MEDIA-MODE.COM

WHY I'VE GOT A PACKER UP MY CLACKER

FIST ON NINE: Media heavyweights and besties James Packer and David Gyngell come to blows in street SEE OUR EXCLUSIVE PICTURES >>P4

HOW TO MAKE YOUR KIDS RICH: MONEYSAVERHQ 〉 Starts P23

- NTNE01Z01MA

GOING TROPPO

THE term 'Going Troppo' could have been coined for the Top End. In fact, Territorians have a season all their own that they call The Troppo Season (also known as The Build-Up).

After a long dry spell, it's a hot, heavy and humid period of weeks before the rains finally fall.

Understandably, for a lot of people, it is their least favourite time of the year. For the editor of the *NT News*, it is your favourite time of the year. The Troppo Season has a funny effect on people.

It makes people who do silly things at other times of the year suddenly start to do *really* silly things. This can sometimes end very badly. Usually in the form of a very laboured pun on the front page of the *NT News*.

DEATH IN PARADISE
Piecing together mum and daughter's deadly holiday

REMEMBERING CYCLONE TRACY

EXCLUSIVE: MCADAM NOW FREE TO PLAY

≫SPORT

GREAT READING IN SATURDAY EXTRA ≫STARTS P15

RUBBER BAN

Casino shuts the door on thong-wearing patrons ≫P2

Bikie links dismissed

THE son of a senior Darwin Hells Angel member has died in Adelaide from multiple stab wounds — but police say there is no connection between the stabbing murder and bikie links.

Kayne David Cluse, 18, died from multiple stab wounds soon after he was driven to the Lyell McEwin Hospital, in Adelaide, on Wednesday night. He is the son of a senior Hells Angel based in Darwin, and the brother of Arron Cluse — a Hells Angels prospect — on trial for allegedly shooting the son of rival bikie Mark Sandery.

⏺ **Full story page 3**

32-PAGE REAL ESTATE LIFTOUT

Property Join the Balmy Army

≫INSIDE TODAY

Fine dogs pensioner

A WOMAN whose 80-year-old dad was fined over the escape of his beloved dog has urged the City of Darwin to show more compassion.

Vicci Reid said her dad Ian Hancock, a pensioner on a walking frame, was unable to chase his maltese pooch Ozzy when he bolted out their front gate — which a carer had left open by mistake — at Malak.

Council dog catchers captured and impounded the seven-year-old dog, who was given to Mr Hancock to keep him company after his wife died. The family was slugged $100 for his release.

⏺ **Full story page 5**

DAVE GARNHAM LIVE TONIGHT @ THE PARAP TAV - 8:30PM!

NT News

YOUR VOICE IN THE TERRITORY

Wednesday, March 13, 2013   ntnews.com.au $1.20 Country freight 20 cents extra   Incl GST

2012 BRAND OF THE YEAR

CRICKET IN CRISIS
LATEST NEWS » SPORT

CROC PULLED OUT OF DARWIN HARBOUR
STORY, PIC » P5

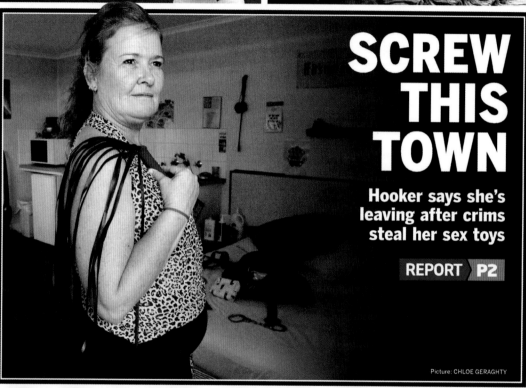

SCREW THIS TOWN

Hooker says she's leaving after crims steal her sex toys

REPORT ▶ P2

Picture: CHLOE GERAGHTY

CONROY GOES TROPPO

A GOVERNMENT appointed enforcer would oversee press standards and have power to apply sanctions that would stifle news reporting, under proposed draconian media changes.

Federal Communications Minister Stephen Conroy yesterday announced the enforcer, given the name Public Interest Media Advocate, among a raft of changes the government will attempt to ram through Parliament by the end of next week.

Former Press Council head David Flint said the changes were dangerous and would "give the government a power it should never have".

◉ STORY: P5

VISIT OUR NEW MOBILE SITE M.NTNEWS.COM.AU TODAY

NORTHERN TERRITORY NEWS

Phone: 8944 9900 CLASSIFIEDS: 8944 9999   DARWIN: Saturday, September 23, 2006 $1.60* (Country Freight / 30 cents extra) Incl. GST

AFL **NRL**

First two
GRAND FINALISTS
decided: *Sport*

Man stabbed with fish

By GREG McLEAN

A MAN is recovering after he was stabbed with the bill of a swordfish measuring almost one metre.

It is believed the 28-year-old victim was drinking with friends when a 26-year-old man, who was with another group, approached him and asked for some beer.

When the man refused, the beer-seeker walked home and collected the swordfish bill — measuring 84cm. He then returned and allegedly used it to stab the first man.

Police believe it is the

Continued Page 5

Motorcyclist dies after city street crash

SPEED and alcohol are believed to have played a part in another tragic fatality on Territory roads yesterday.

Damian James Mitchell, 21, died in Royal Darwin Hospital after crashing his motorbike in Larrakeyah.

The accident happened about 4am as Mr Mitchell was travelling along Mitchell St before colliding with a traffic sign at the Lambell Tce intersection.

Heavy rain was pelting down at the time of the accident.

Witnesses told police they saw Mr Mitchell leave a nightclub and ride down Mitchell St, Darwin city, in slippery conditions at excessive speed.

Police also believe he may have swerved to avoid hitting a pedestrian before the crash. They have appealed for that person to come forward with any information that

Continued Page 2

TRAGEDY: This is the mangled wreckage of the bike Damian Mitchell was riding. Picture: DANI GAWLIK

NT News

Monday, July 8, 2013   ntnews.com.au $1.20 Country freight 20 cents extra Incl GST

2012 BRAND OF THE YEAR

KICKED OFF THE BUS FOR RUDE SHIRT
WHAT DID IT SAY? »P3

ALL THE AFL & NRL ACTION
JUST FOOTY LIFTOUT

WORLD'S BIGGEST PYRAMID TO BE BUILT IN THE TERRITORY

But there's a catch... it's going to be made from toxic rocks

NORTHERN TERRITORY (350 m)

EGYPT (138.8 m)

MEXICO (30 m)

FULL STORY   **P2**

Image digitally altered
Artist: STUART THORNTON

DINGO ATTACKS, EATS PET DOG

STORY, SHOCKING PICTURE »P2

RESIDENTS FEAR THEIR CHILDREN COULD BE NEXT

NT News

YOUR VOICE IN THE TERRITORY

Newspaper 2010 PANPA AWARDS Of The Year

Saturday, July 2, 2011

ntnews.com.au

$1.60 Country freight 30 cents extra Incl GST

Man arrested after cops spot suspiciously small package in his undies

INSIDE FULL STORY »P2

PARKING METER MAIDS FOR DARWIN STREETS ›P3

SUNDAY 1PM TREV TRAVOLTA'S @ TRAILER BOAT CLUB

NT★News

YOUR VOICE IN THE TERRITORY

Thursday, October 31, 2013   ntnews.com.au $1.20 Country freight 50cents extra Incl GST

WIN A TRIP TO MARGARET RIVER

CODE WORD ≫P18

TOURIST'S EERIE PREMONITION BEFORE NT DEATH

FULL STORY ≫P3

ZINGER BURGLAR

Fast food bandit walks free from jail for being wrongly accused of KFC robbery ... and is arrested within minutes for allegedly robbing another KFC store

FULL STORY ≫ **P2**

NT★News

YOUR VOICE IN THE TERRITORY

Friday, August 3, 2012

ntnews.com.au

$1.20 Country freight 20cents extra Incl GST

Last year Territorians drank the equivalent of ...

6.1 MILLION CARTONS OF HEAVY BEER

The good news is we're cutting down

REPORT > P2

2012 Darwin Cup Special
OFFICE SWEEP
>> INSIDE TODAY P16, FULL RACING COVERAGE: SPORT

DR ELEPHANT LIVE TONIGHT @ PARAP TAVERN!!

SUNDAY Territorian

Sunday, January 7, 2007

$1.30* (Country Freight 20 cents extra) Incl. GST

Our Brooke sizzles – P3
+ full-colour poster P21

BINGO
your chance to win $12,000: P6

Territory jet truck burns up Summernats: Full story P2

Ice cream

SWEET: Similar ice creams to those stolen yesterday

bandit caught cold-handed

A SWEET-toothed thief who allegedly stole more than 30 ice creams from a service station was caught cold by police before he could eat them.

Police said yesterday the 27-year-old "had made off with an armful of Cornetto ice creams, of all things".

Continued Page 2

Three pages of great New Year's Eve social photos: P59-61

NORTHERN TERRITORY NEWS

Phone: 8944 9900   CLASSIFIEDS: 8944 9999   DARWIN: Friday, April 15, 2005 $1.00* (Country Freight 20 cents extra) Incl. GST

Jack Ah Quit
NT minister to step down: P3

Sex worker killers to appeal: P5

Taxpayers fund bondage workshop

By PAUL DYER

Territory taxpayers funded sadomasochism and bondage workshops, it was revealed last night.

The *Northern Territory News* has learned a $2500 grant was given to the Sex Worker Outreach Project (SWOP).

It was spent on three workshops on "bondage discipline and sadomasochistic practice".

Attended by Top End sex workers, the three-hour workshops were held late last year at Brown's Mart in Darwin.

They were hosted by two Brisbane experts — Mr Big Pants and Mistress Natasha.

The *Northern Territory News* obtained a copy of the SWOP newsletter, which is marked "not for general distribution or display".

It states: "Mistress Natasha shared her skills on sexy sexually transmitted infection checks.

"(She) had a lot of props and

Continued: Page 2

Cool ... Rod Harris (left) and Stuart Park firie Jim Bury yesterday. Picture: PATRINA MALONE

Snow place like foam in the Territory

By GREG McLEAN

Alaskan firefighter Rod Harris is feeling right at home in the Northern Territory — especially when he cops the odd "snowball" from workmates.

As part of an exchange that saw the Anchorage native swap roles with Territory firefighter Phil Karlhuber for 12 months, Mr Harris landed in Darwin two weeks ago with wife Jami and their three children ready for some Top End action. "All I brought with me was two pairs of shorts and three T-shirts," he said. "We all feel right at home already."

So while Mr Karlhuber and his

Continued: Page 3

YOUR VOICE IN THE TERRITORY

NT News

Monday, September 9, 2013   ntnews.com.au $1.20 Country freight 20 cents extra Incl GST

TREASURE CHEST

MYSTERY OF THE MISSING LINGERIE REVEALED P2

PICTURE: KATRINA BRIDGEFORD

BUMPER MUNDIE UNDIE EDITION

WHY DID THE CROC CROSS THE ROAD

FULL STORY
Page 3

ELECTION 2013
THE TERRITORY HAS SPOKEN

FULL COVERAGE P8-9

NORTHERN TERRITORY NEWS

Phone: 8944 9900 CLASSIFIEDS: 8944 9999   DARWIN: Wednesday, September 13, 2006 $1.10* (Country Freight 20 cents extra) Incl. GST

NT kids' tribute to their hero, Steve Irwin

2 pages of their pictures, letters, poems: P14,15

Bumbling Brit gets lost again ... in the *same* spot

WHERE'S WALLY?

LAST TUESDAY: RESCUED AFTER 3 DAYS

YESTERDAY: RESCUED AFTER 4 DAYS

By GREG McLEAN and LEE STEBHENS

A TOURIST dubbed the "Bumbling Brit" after getting lost for three days on the edge of a Territory town last week, has done it again.

Martin Lake, 50, a former trainee policeman from Birkenhead in England, was labelled the Bumbling Brit in the UK media just last week after spending three days lost on the edge of Alice Springs.

Alice Springs Bowling Club worker Rosemary Packham was yesterday dumbfounded after being told Mr Lake was apparently lost for a second time.

"He's a Wally," she said. "Surely you wouldn't be that silly to go and do the same thing again."

The Bumbling Brit yesterday sparked his second large scale search – involving three helicopters conservatively estimated to have cost Territory taxpayers $10,000 – after becoming lost in the same area again.

Police, Emergency Services volunteers and park rangers also took part in a ground search – as they did last time. Alice Springs Watch Commander Senior Sergeant Michael Potts said rescuers found Mr Lake late yesterday – after he had been missing for four days this time.

"He was found in a slightly different location, approximately 4.6km from town," he said. The hotel where Mr Lake was staying raised the alarm after the British tourist failed to check out last Friday.

Continued Page 2

> He's a Wally. Surely you wouldn't be that silly

NORTHERN TERRITORY NEWS

Phone: 8944 9900 Classifieds: 8944 9999 www.ntnews.com.au

Tuesday, December 16, 2008

$1.20* (Country freight 20 cents extra) Incl. GST

COP THIS
Police officers stood down over Hookers Ball photos

By REBEKAH CAVANAGH

TWO Northern Territory police officers caught in compromising positions with scantily-clad women while they were meant to be on duty patrolling the streets have been stood down from operational duties.

These photographs obtained

Continued Page 2

MORE PIX INSIDE

CYCLONE TIPPED FOR THIS WEEK

AWASH: Pedestrians caught in a Darwin downpour yesterday ... the weather bureau says a lot more is on the way

By NADJA HAINKE

THERE is a high chance that a tropical cyclone will develop off the north coast of Australia this week.

The weather bureau has issued a tropical cyclone outlook, saying the chance for a cyclone to develop on Thursday was high — 50 per cent or more.

A monsoon trough lies just off the north coast, with a tropical low located in the Timor Sea — about 400km north of Darwin.

The low has a 10 per cent chance to develop into a cyclone today. And the risk could increase by Thursday.

But severe weather forecaster Todd Smith said the Top End was not under threat.

"Cyclones are very unpredictable systems but at this stage there is no guidance that the cyclone would threaten Darwin," he said. Mr Smith said the low was slow moving.

But he said it was expected to develop and move towards the west or southwest where it could form into a cyclone around the Kimberley region.

Despite the distance, Darwin's weather would be affected by the development.

"Over the next few days, as the low develops over the Timor Sea, we will see an increase in squally showers and rainfall," he said. "We will see some large waves and certainly some

Continued Page 5

MINISTRY "ANNUAL" TOUR DISCOVERY THUR

NT★News

YOUR VOICE IN THE TERRITORY

Saturday, July 7, 2012 ntnews.com.au $1.60 Country freight 30 cents extra Incl GST

IT'S SHOW TIME IN ALICE

REPORT, PICS » P6

Hen Wendy Haddon with one of the officers who showed up at the Humpty Doo Hotel

TO PERVE AND PROTECT

Police mistaken for strippers at Top End hen's night

REPORT ▸ P2

FIRE STARTED BY CIGARETTE DESTROYS THREE HOMES ▸ P7

NT THUNDER VS ASPLEY HORNETS AT TIO STADIUM 6PM

NORTHERN TERRITORY NEWS

Phone: 8944 9900 CLASSIFIEDS: 8944 9999   DARWIN: Thursday, June 21, 2007 $1.10* (Country Freight 20 cents extra) Incl. GST

3 DAYS OF THUNDER
Special 10th Anniversary
V8 Supercar 12-page liftout
ALL THE DRIVERS, CARS AND HIDDEN VALLEY MAP

BLOODY FREEZING

Coldest Top End June day ever recorded

By REBEKAH CAVANAGH

BLOODY hell. Anybody would think we were in Melbourne.

Rugged-up Darwin residents yesterday shivered through the coldest daytime-high temperature ever recorded in June – and the second equal coldest day on record in the city. At 1pm the mercury plummeted to 22.7C — and

unseasonally strong winds made it even harder to keep warm.

While southerners would probably look on in envy as they shivered though single-digit temperatures, many Darwinites resorted to pulling out their rarely-sighted winter woolies.

The daytime high was only 1.6C above the coldest day ever

Continued Page 3

BRRRRRR: The Darwin daytime temperature near its 'high' yesterday and (INSET) winds sank this boat at Tipperary Waters

Demerit points:
'Double or nothing' licence chances

By BEN LANGFORD

TERRITORY drivers will be able to play a game of "double or nothing" if they have their licences suspended under the new demerit points scheme.

Motorists will have their licence suspended if they lose 12 demerit points over three years. But they will be able to choose to enter a 12-month good behaviour period where they can keep driving.

If they lose two points in that time they will serve double the original licence suspension. Driving at less than 15km/h over the limit will lead to only one point docked, which in effect means motorists will have a second chance to speed before they lose their licence.

The Automobile Association of the Northern Territory said it supported the NT Government's road safety package – but the demerit points should be tougher.

General manager Linda Deans said: "They haven't

Continued Page 2

MANHUNT OVER
Suspect bikie gives up: P11

LEGISLATION
NT moves on paintball: P2

NT⬥News

YOUR VOICE IN THE TERRITORY

Tuesday, August 17, 2010   ntnews.com.au   Country freight 20 cents extra   Incl GST **$1.20**

Picture: Brad Fleet

INSIDE › MILLS STANDS FIRM AGAINST CLP REVOLT: **P4**

SEXY GRANNY DROUGHT

By ALYSSA BETTS

MOBS of sexy grannies in their 60s or so can save Darwin from the Groundhog Day exodus that strips the city of brains and money every few decades, a Territory demographer said.

Charles Darwin Univers-

ity's Dr Dean Carson warns the folk who swarmed to the NT after Cyclone Tracy and self-government will soon be popping off back down south.

They're the "young olds" who take with them up to a million bucks in super and

↻ Continued p2

MAMBO TUESDAY CLARKE CENTRAL LIVE @ MONSOONS

NORTHERN TERRITORY NEWS

BUMPER 72 PAGES

Phone: 8944 9900 Classifieds: 8944 9999 www.ntnews.com.au

Wednesday, March 31, 2010

$1.20* (Country freight 20 cents extra) Incl. GST

WIN a ride on a superbike >>P68

Sic' em, Rex

HE WAS the fearsome rogue Territory croc who once ate everything from pet dogs to his own potential lovers.

But when the former lady killer finally managed to eat just one chicken, it was cause for enormous celebration.

Full story *PLUS*
Croc still on loose near Darwin school >>P8,9

Restaurant charges 'thongage'

By **BEN LANGFORD**

A DARWIN restaurant is charging patrons $10 for wearing thongs while they dine.

The "thongage" charge is announced in a sign on the door of

Continued Page 3

THONGAGE
Surcharge $10-00
Monday To Saturday

NT News

YOUR VOICE IN THE TERRITORY

Tuesday, March 27, 2012   ntnews.com.au   **$1.20** Country fringe 20cents extra Incl GST

HOLDING OUT FOR A HIRO

NEW FISHING COLUMN »P39

MY BALI JAIL NIGHTMARE

STORY »P9

DOGS OF PHWOAARR!

Thousands of Territorians have taken up a bizarre sex craze called dogging, using the ruse of walking their pooch as cover for going out to have sex with strangers in public

FULL REPORT P2

TOO RUDE

Picture: DANIEL HARTLEY-ALLEN

Win Free Flights

HOW TO WIN »P7

2NITE HOOPERS T.O.T. BEACH PARTY @ HP

NORTHERN TERRITORY NEWS.

Still only $1.20*

Phone: 8944 9900 Classifieds: 8944 9999 www.ntnews.com.au

Wednesday, February 10, 2010

$1.20* (Country freight 20 cents extra) Incl. GST

New daily TV guide has more channels
DETAILS >>P21

Pressure takes toll on Gerry
FULL STORY >>P7

Win a Thai holiday with your Valentine's message
FIND OUT HOW >>P16

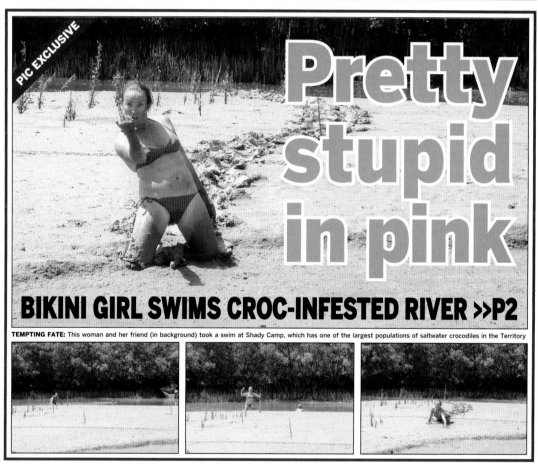

PIC EXCLUSIVE

Pretty stupid in pink

BIKINI GIRL SWIMS CROC-INFESTED RIVER >>P2

TEMPTING FATE: This woman and her friend (in background) took a swim at Shady Camp, which has one of the largest populations of saltwater crocodiles in the Territory

BABE NATION TONITE @ THE VIC

NT News

YOUR VOICE IN THE TERRITORY

Thursday, February 13, 2014   ntnews.com.au $1.20 Country freight 20 cents extra Incl GST

POKIE LAWS STOP FLOOD VICTIMS BUYING FOOD

DETAILS ≫P5

NT AVOIDS NATION'S MAN DROUGHT CRISIS

REPORT ≫P3

Picture: PATRINA MALONE

OH TRUCK ... WE'RE STUCK

FIND OUT WHAT HAPPENED ▷ P2

POLLIE, WHAT A SLACKER

ARE OUR ELECTED MEMBERS AUSTRALIA'S LAZIEST?

FULL STORY ≫P2

12-PAGE NT Business Review INSIDE   **MR. MEN BOOK TOKEN ⟩ P2**

NT★News

YOUR VOICE IN THE TERRITORY

Saturday, July 24, 2010 ntnews.com.au $1.60 Country freight 30 cents extra Incl GST

GONE TROPPO

1 Naked man flees after caught swimming in posh hotel pool

2 30 youths in wild street brawl before police chase

3 Police called to 480 jobs as full moon closes in

INSIDE > Read about Darwin's night of madness: **P4**
Have your say: **ntnews.com.au**

Picture: BRAD FLEET

COOKING DEMOS EVERY SAT 11-1 DARWIN FISH MARKET

PLANES, TRAINS AND AUTOMOBILES

THE Territory is a big place with not many people in it. It takes four hours – or, in most cases, a lot, lot longer – to drive from one town to the next.

So it is understandable that Territorians have a very close relationship with their vehicles. In some cases – such as the guy who police pulled over for speeding at 150km/h while filming himself masturbating at the wheel of his car, which was laden with drugs, a loaded firearm and a couple of cannabis plants – too close.

So, the phrase 'going all the way' can often mean more than just getting between points A and B when using transport in the Territory.

Just ask the bloke behind the headline 'Trouser Snake on a Plane' or the amorous female boatie and her partner who showed other anglers they enjoyed getting their tackle out and their clothing off while cruising down the river.

All very moving stories.

NT☀News

YOUR VOICE IN THE TERRITORY

Saturday, February 1, 2014   ntnews.com.au $2 Country freight 30 cents extra* Incl GST

BACK IN BLACK

Today the Territory returns to open speed limits >>P2

NT ● News

YOUR VOICE IN THE TERRITORY

Wednesday, October 6, 2010   ntnews.com.au $1.20 Country freight 30cents extra Incl GST

2010 PANPA AWARDS Newspaper Of The Year

AGONY and the ECSTASY
GAMES WRAP: SPORT

This paper can save you money
DISCOUNT COUPON: P3

DRIVING MR LAZY

INSIDE ❯ Car chaise at Mindil Beach ❯❯ P2

HAMBURGLAR

Jilted lover jailed after breaking into ex's house, burning $8000 of her clothes ... then settling in to cook himself some hamburgers > STORY P2

COUGAR PARTY LOST ARC THIS FRIDAY NITE

NT★News

YOUR VOICE IN THE TERRITORY

Wednesday, May 30, 2012 | ntnews.com.au | $1.20 Country freight 20cents extra Incl GST

SELL YOUR STUFF FOR FREE
$500 FLEA MARKET LIMIT ≫P3

IT'S BLOODY FREEZING
HOW COLD WAS IT? ≫P5

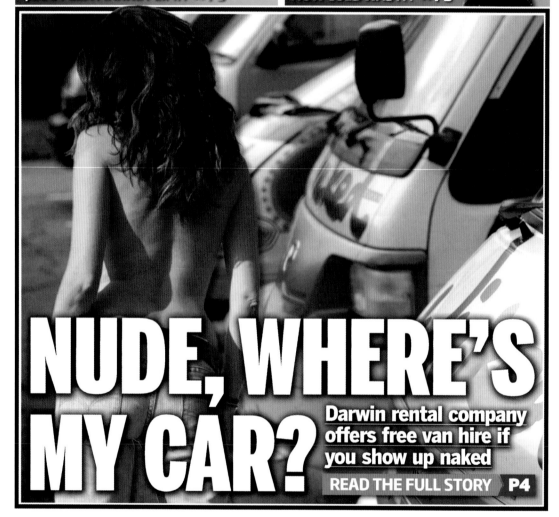

NUDE, WHERE'S MY CAR?

Darwin rental company offers free van hire if you show up naked

READ THE FULL STORY **P4**

NORTHERN TERRITORY NEWS

Phone: 8944 9900 Classifieds: 8944 9999 www.ntnews.com.au — Friday, January 11, 2008 — $1.20* (Country freight 20 cents extra) Incl. GST

CARBOOM

HOT ROD: NEWSBREAKER Territory policeman Sen-Sgt Trevor Howie took this photo just as gas bottles exploded between the four-wheel-drive and the caravan

Family of five lucky to escape from highway fireball

By DANIEL BOURCHIER

A FAMILY of five was lucky to survive when their four-wheel-drive exploded into flames.

Their caravan and all their possessions were also destroyed.

The 78-year-old driver, two women, aged 74 and 34, a man aged 33 and a two-year-old boy managed to get out before the fire took full hold.

They told police they had switched the Pajero from gas to petrol and the motor started to splutter before the vehicle stopped. When the engine was restarted, flames and smoke billowed from the engine.

The near-disaster happened on the Stuart Highway at the McLaren Creek crossing, 70km south of Tennant Creek, at 3pm on Wednesday.

Police Senior Sergeant Trevor Howie was the first officer on the scene. The former Tennant Creek officer had been in the town for a court case and was returning to Alice Springs.

"I could see a large ball of smoke in the air," he said.

"A driver had blocked the southern part of the road and when I saw a man in the drain, I ran up and made sure there was no-one in the car.

"I arranged for other travellers to look after him — he had **Continued Page 2**

EXCLUSIVE: Drivers caught on drugs will keep licences

By MATT CUNNINGHAM

MOTORISTS caught drug-driving will keep their licences and not be hit with demerit points under laws expected to be passed in Parliament next month.

First-time offenders will be let off with a slap on the wrist — a $200 fine and no loss of licence.

Drivers caught for a second time face a fine of up to $750 and three months loss of licence, and subsequent offenders will lose their licences for six months and be fined up to $750. But demerit point losses will not apply to any drug-driving offence.

The Territory is the last jurisdiction in Australia to introduce drug testing for motorists. The Drug Driving Bill was introduced into **Continued Page 3**

Pitbull that mauled young boy 'had attacked before'

By KASEY BRUNT

A DOG that mauled a 12-year-old boy in a friend's yard had attacked before, it was revealed yesterday.

The pitbull attacked Zac McPhillips while he was playing on Wednesday.

His 10-year-old brother Jordan had also been savaged by the same dog. The pitbull has been put down.

The boys' mother, Joanne Humphrey, said she was angered it had not been destroyed after the first attack.

"We had to take Jordan to the hospital a month ago and we are here now with Zac," she said yesterday.

"We really thought they would have put the dog down the first time."

Zac, who was playing in the Darwin suburb of Anula **Continued Page 3**

NT★News

YOUR VOICE IN THE TERRITORY

Tuesday, February 4, 2014   ntnews.com.au $1.20 Country freight 20 cents extra Incl GST

MASSIVE HIKE IN GROG TAXES

FULL STORY ≫P3

MEASLES PUT TWO IN INTENSIVE CARE

DETAILS ≫P3

Video online

ntnews .com.au

FOOL SPEED AHEAD

AMAZING FOOTAGE OF IDIOT 'SURFING' HIS BOAT

READ THE FULL STORY ≫ P2

NT'S BIGGEST POLITICAL DONORS

REVEALED ≫P4

KING TIDES, CYCLONES AND LOTS OF RAIN

WEATHER WRAP ≫P5

NORTHERN TERRITORY NEWS

Phone: 8944 9900 Classifieds: 8944 9999 www.ntnews.com.au

Tuesday, November 18, 2008

$1.20* (Country freight 20 cents extra) Incl. GST

PART 4 TODAY
CYCLONE TERRITORY
LIFTOUT >> PAGE 15

MORE HORROR
PATIENT WAKES UP DURING SURGERY
EXCLUSIVE >> PAGE 3

IT'S HERE
FINALLY...
THE PREMIERE
STORY >> PAGE 5

IS THIS SEAT SHAKIN'? Lucas Knudson leaves court yesterday

Trouser snake on a plane

Is this bloke a complete tosser?
Court told driver fined for indecent masturbating... at 15cm/s

Handyman fined for obscene act on Virgin

By PHOEBE STEWART

A MAN who described himself as a "jack of all trades" has been fined for exposing himself and masturbating in front of a woman on a Darwin-bound flight.

Lucas Steven Knudson argued he was "just adjusting himself" because his jeans were too tight, a Darwin court heard yesterday.

The case follows hot on the heels of a recent front page *NT News* report *(pictured above)* in

Continued Page 2

YOU MUDDY IDIOT! Streaker almost killed at mud racing

By REBEKAH CAVANAGH

A STREAKER cheated death by the skin of his teeth when he made a naked dash through the Top End Mud Racing track in the middle of an event.

The 19-year-old man jumped the 2m-high fence and ran across the arena before "swan-diving" in a thigh-deep pool of muddy water on the racing circuit in front of a huge crowd at Downes Park on Saturday night. Officials stopped the mud racers roaring around the track moments before they were to plough through the puddle he was prancing around in.

It was the first time in mud racing history there had been a streaker. Top End Mud Racing Association president Chris Lovewell said the man was "extremely lucky".

"He was less than 20m away from being dead," he said.

"The drivers have very limited vision and had we not managed to stop the car mid-race it would have ploughed through the water and straight over the top of him.

"And if the driver had hit that person they wouldn't have even known until they got back in the pits." Mr Lovewell said the stunt was "stupid" and that the association would not tolerate that sort of behaviour at the popular family event. "We're 100 per cent against it," he said.

"It's not like at a football match where it is all fun and games.

"When you are dealing with any motorsport it is a potentially deadly

Continued Page 3

MANHUNT FINALISTS AT CROC COVE 4PM 2DAY

NORTHERN TERRITORY NEWS

Phone 8944 9900 CLASSIFIEDS: 8944 9999   DARWIN: Friday, June 28, 2002 $1.00* (Country Freight 20 cents extra) Incl. GST

DRY HUMOUR - YOUR JOKES
THE LAUGH IS ON US
ANOTHER WINNER, SELECTION OF GAGS - P6,7

MOTHER DEFENDS SLINGSHOT ATHLETE
PAGE 5

OOPS

100-tonne train derails two years before track finished

End of the line ... the scene at the Katherine sleeper plant yesterday

By CAMDEN SMITH
Political Reporter

A multimillion-dollar, 100-tonne locomotive crashed off the track on the Alice Springs to Darwin railway yesterday.

It is the first derailment on the $1.3 billion line – two years before the railway is due to be opened.

The locomotive, which was pulling six 70-tonne wagons, overshot the end of the line at the Katherine sleeper plant yesterday morning.

Embarrassed ADrail staff said the derailment would be investigated.

Project construction manager Kevyn Brown said the crash had only a minimal impact on work at the site, which was the starting point of ADrail's Top End construction operations.

He said the driver, whose name he would not release, was the only passenger on the locomotive and was unhurt.

Mr Brown said ADrail had other locomotives that would be deployed to cover for the missing engine.

"The locomotive was pulling towards the end of the line in Katherine and it came off the rail at the end of the track," he told the *Northern Territory News*.

Continued, Page 2
Wicking, Page 12

F-111s grounded after Darwin landing: P2

NT★News

YOUR VOICE IN THE TERRITORY

Thursday, November 11, 2010 ntnews.com.au $1.20 Country freight 20 cents extra Incl GST

Newspaper 2010 PANPA AWARDS of The Year

ALL TOADS LEAD TO PALMO

Council surrenders in the war against cane toads

INSIDE ▶ FULL STORY: P4

Picture: BRAD FLEET

Find out how the NT went in the **NATIONAL IQ TEST** ≫P2

FLO RIDA DISCOVERY SAT 27 NOV ON SALE NOW

YOUR VOICE IN THE TERRITORY

NT★News

Thursday, September 15, 2011   ntnews.com.au $1.20 Country freight 20 cents extra Incl GST

Having your car towed is one thing but ...

READER PIC

THIS IS FORKED

Builders use forklift to shift vehicles from street   EXCLUSIVE ≫P2

NT News

YOUR VOICE IN THE TERRITORY

Thursday, April 3, 2014   ntnews.com.au $1.20 Country freight 20 cents extra Incl GST

CIRCUS 1
KIDS LEARN TRICKS OF THE TRADE
STORY ≫P3

CIRCUS 2
GILES: I WON'T BE PART OF THE SIDESHOW
REPORT ≫P7

SORRY DAD, I BORROWED YOUR CAR BUT...
Find out how it happened ≫P2

SAILOR BASHED FOR CHEESEBURGER

FULL STORY ≫P2

GARDENS' TRIPLE TREAT
ENTERTAINMENT LIFTOUT ≫P15

WIN 1 OF 10 FAMILY MOVIE PASSES
DETAILS ≫P14

NORTHERN TERRITORY NEWS

Still only

Phone: 8944 9900 Classifieds: 8944 9999 www.ntnews.com.au

Saturday, October 10, 2009

$1.60* (Country freight 30 cents extra) Incl. GST

You could share in more than $5 million

Lucky codeword and how to enter > P3

CRASH VICTIM tells

"I did *NOT* have sexual relations with that driver!"

BLOWN OUT OF PROPORTION: Allyson White strenuously denies a police report she was involved in "amorous activities" with the driver of this ute when it crashed.

STORY: P4

Picture: FIONA MORRISON

P2
Glasser guilty

A FORMER prison guard has been found guilty of glassing a Darwin soldier. The victim lost an eye after Te Tuhi Puru Westrupp slammed a beer glass in his face at Lost Arc.

P24
Exclusive extract

UNDERWORLD celebrity Mick Gatto is a man who has experienced many lines of work, his latest incarnation is as an author. Read our exclusive extract from his new book.

P88
Fevola now a Lion

CONTROVERSY continues to plague AFL star Brendan Fevola, with a sexual assault claim emerging as he was traded to Brisbane and its fearsome forward line.

P88
Bathurst or bust

V8 SUPERCARS' Ford star Craig Lowndes is chasing a fourth straight Bathurst crown but Holden driver Jason Richards has qualified fastest for today's top 10 shootout.

TREV TREVOLTAS LIVE @ BEACHFRONT 2NITE

YOUR VOICE IN THE TERRITORY

NT★News

Monday, June 24, 2013   ntnews.com.au $1.20 Country freight 20 cents extra Incl GST

2012 BRAND OF THE YEAR

TRUCKING IDIOT

INSIDE ❯ **READ THE FULL STORY P2**

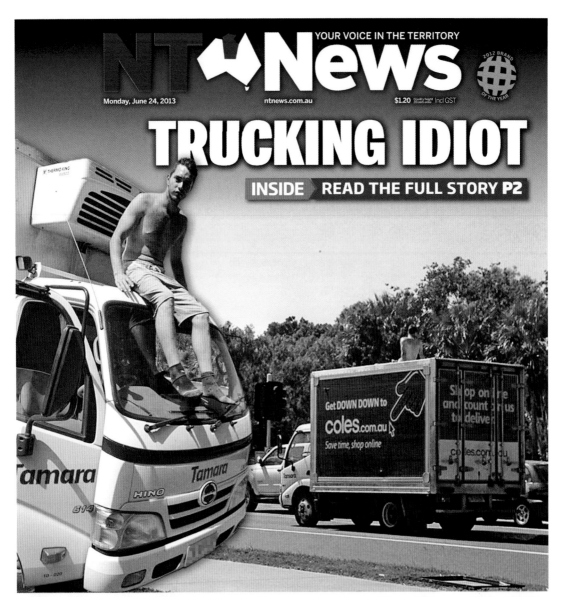

Get DOWN DOWN to
coles.com.au
Save time, shop online

Shop online
and count on us
to deliver
coles.com.au

Tamara
HINO

DAY OF CHAOS ON TERRITORY ROADS

FIVE CRASHES CREATE MAYHEM » FULL REPORT P2

NORTHERN TERRITORY NEWS

Phone: 8944 9900 Classifieds: 8944 9999 www.ntnews.com.au   **Thursday, July 31, 2008** $1.20* (Country freight 20 cents extra) Incl. GST

MOTORCYCLIST KILLED ON FOGGY ROADS

Story >> P5

WIN a $4475 boat and motor package

Proudly Supplied By... Territory Marine

Today's token, details >> P25

Is this bloke a complete tosser?

Court told driver filmed himself masturbating ... at 150km/h

By PHOEBE STEWART

A TERRITORY man filmed himself speeding at 150km/h while masturbating at the wheel of his drug-laden car, a court heard.

His Holden SV6 was allegedly laden with 5kg of drugs, including two cannabis plants resting on the back seat, the court was told.

Brendon Alan Erhardt *(pictured)*, 39, was granted bail so he could marry

Continued Page 2

NT◆News

YOUR VOICE IN THE TERRITORY

Friday, January 31, 2014   ntnews.com.au $1.20 Country freight 20 cents extra Incl GST

THORPEY IN REHAB

REPORT »**P3**

FALCONIO: TV SHOW'S THREE-YEAR-OLD 'EXCLUSIVE'

FULL STORY »**P2**

DUD ROUTE

Is this the nation's worst bus terminal? »**P2**

WOMEN'S ROUND: LATEESHA KEEPS IT IN THE FAMILY ⟩ **JUST FOOTY**

YOUR VOICE IN THE TERRITORY

NT News

Wednesday, September 5, 2012   ntnews.com.au $1.20 Country freight 30 cents extra Incl GST

Government appoints nine new department heads after sacking six > P3

CAR POOL

Drunk driver finds himself in the deep end

FULL STORY > P2

A driver lost control of his Toyota Camry wagon, crashing through a fence

Picture: BRAD FLEET

ALL THE LATEST CELEBRITY GOSSIP

CHECK OUT CONFIDENTIAL >> P20-21

TERRITORY'S PRIDE AND JOY

PRIDE OF AUSTRALIA WINNERS >> P4-5

NT ✦ News

YOUR VOICE IN THE TERRITORY

Wednesday, February 5, 2014   ntnews.com.au $1.20 Country freight (Darwin extra) Incl GST

TWO FINED IN NEW OPEN SPEED AREAS
REPORT »P7

THREAT TO DOCK NT FIRIES PAY
REVEALED »P5

21 BUM SALUTE

OUR CHEEKY WELCOME TO MARK GHAN'S 10th YEAR »P2

Picture: JUSTIN SANSON

MY BALI NIGHTMARE

DARWIN WOMAN'S TRIP FROM HELL
EXCLUSIVE ⟩ P4

CYCLONE TO MERGE WITH NT LOW ⟩ FULL STORY PAGE 3

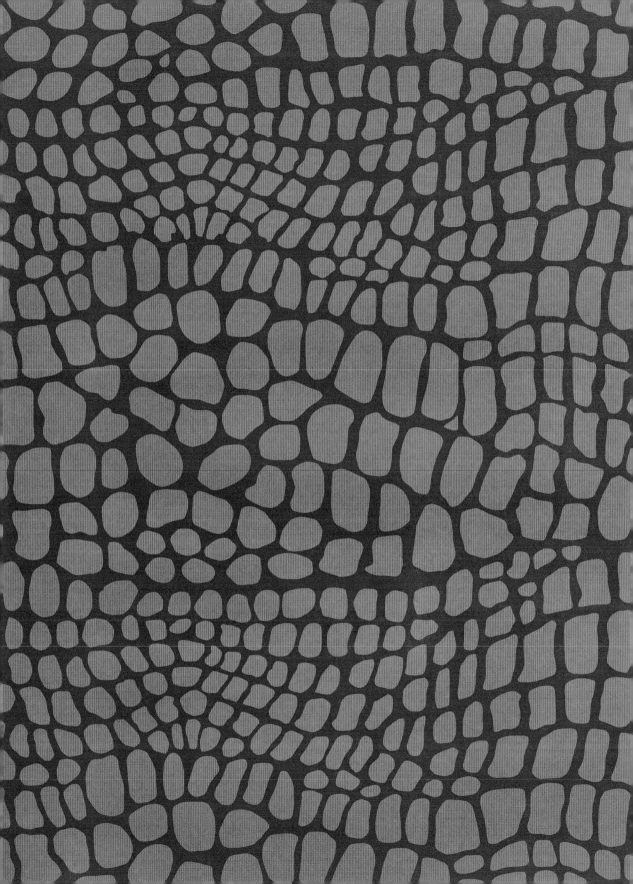

THE TRUTH IS
UP THERE

'I WANT to believe that there's intelligent life up there!'

No, that's not Agent Fox Mulder talking about the existence of aliens and UFOs. That's some tweed-jacket-wearing southern media commentator talking about the *NT News*' Darwin-based editorial staff after they chose to put yet another UFO, or alien, or yowie story on their front page.

It's not our fault that the beautiful Top End attracts more interesting characters than the boring south does. And come on . . . why wouldn't we share their incredible stories with our readers?

Seriously, if you're the *NT News* editor and you don't put a story about a horny ghost on Page 1 then it's time to hand in your autographed videotape of the Roswell autopsy.

Forget your Area 51, America – we've got our own Area 69 right here in the Territory.

NT News

YOUR VOICE IN THE TERRITORY

Thursday, September 30, 2010   ntnews.com.au $1.20 Country freight 20 cents extra Incl GST

PANPA 2010 AWARDS Newspaper of The Year

HORNY GHOST HAUNTS HOUSE

If you thought Casper was friendly, you should meet Kevin

INSIDE Annie Sanson's exclusive story: **P2**

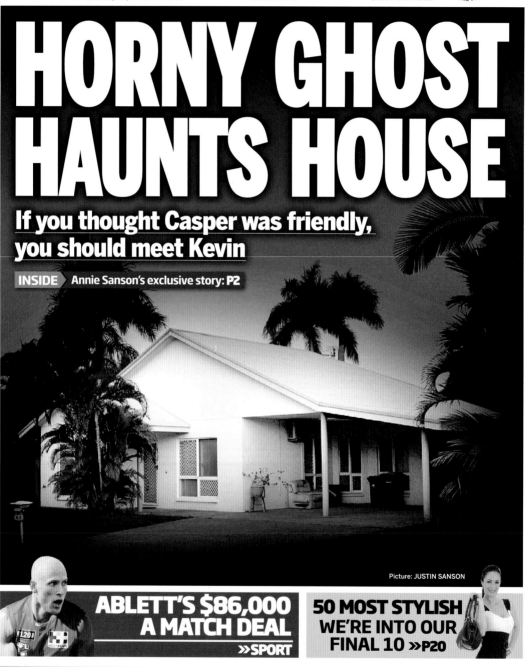

Picture: JUSTIN SANSON

ABLETT'S $86,000 A MATCH DEAL
»SPORT

50 MOST STYLISH WE'RE INTO OUR FINAL 10 »P20

NORTHERN TERRITORY NEWS

Phone: 8944 9900 Classifieds: 8944 9999   www.ntnews.com.au   **Saturday, January 17, 2009** $1.60* (Country freight 30 cents extra) Incl. GST

'Flying car' UFO over Darwin

By ALYSSA BETTS

A MYSTERIOUS blue car-shaped UFO has been spotted in Darwin as it flew across a cloudy wet season sky.

But in the words of amateur photographer Mark Schmutter, 79, "It does look like a car but what

Continued Page 5

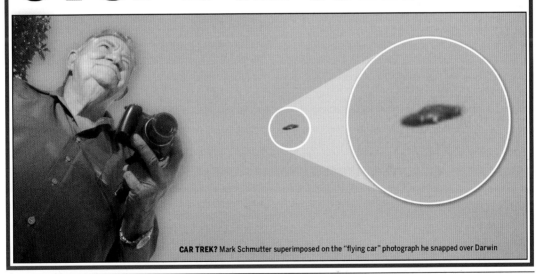

CAR TREK? Mark Schmutter superimposed on the "flying car" photograph he snapped over Darwin

FIND OUT FIRST WWW.NTNEWS.COM.AU

NT★News

YOUR VOICE IN THE TERRITORY

Saturday, September 11, 2010   ntnews.com.au $1.60 Country freight 30 cents extra Incl GST

ABC host discovers The Truth is Out There

It's not a question of "Is there anything out there?" More like "just what is out there?" That's what Leon Compton discovered after callers swamped his show with UFO stories

FULL STORY »P2

Picture: STUART WALMSLEY

Driver: Station wagon-shaped spaceship pulled alongside us

UFO CUT OFF MY CAR

INSIDE

Witnesses tell of their sightings: P2

MISS INDY GRAND FINAL @ THE VIC TONITE 11PM

NT News

YOUR VOICE IN THE TERRITORY

Thursday, October 10, 2013   ntnews.com.au $1.20 Country freight 20 cents extra Incl GST

2012 BRAND OF THE YEAR

CHOPPER'S LAST STAND

REPORT ≫ **P11**

SENTENCED TO A JOB

≫ **NT BUSINESS REVIEW LIFTOUT**

KILLER'S EX RUNS FOR COUNCIL

INSIDE

READ THE FULL REPORT ≫ P2

IMAGE DIGITALLY ALTERED

ALIEN ALERT

Are UFOs abducting Territorians? Our resident ufologist has evidence to say they are ≫ **P4**

THIS SUN-BOY@BEAR/GRINSPOON/RUFUS/ SULTAN- SKI CLUB

NT News

YOUR VOICE IN THE TERRITORY

2012 BRAND OF THE YEAR

Friday, August 16, 2013 · ntnews.com.au · $1.20 Country freight 20 cents extra Incl GST

McHAPPY MEAL LURES ESCAPED TEENS FROM ROOF
REPORT **»P7**

WIN TICKETS TO SEE TIMOMATIC IN SYDNEY
DETAILS **»P18**

PM GOES TROPPO

Rudd's bold plan to turn Top End into tax haven, but who will pay? P4-5

*Picture not digitally altered

Picture: MICHAEL FRANCHI

WITCHES SAVED BY AN ELF
FULL STORY ▸ **P2**

Attorney-General John Elferink gets his witch on as he prepares to repeal a 300-year witchcraft act

NT**News**

YOUR VOICE IN THE TERRITORY

Wednesday, July 28, 2010   ntnews.com.au $1.20 Country freight 30 cents extra Incl GST

CHECK OUT THE NEW LOOK
UNDERBELLY STAR HITS NT »19

$50,000 IN FLIGHTS TO WIN
DETAILS »16

Jet

FREE ENTRY TO TODAY'S RACES WITH OUR COUPON » 3

IS THIS THE
TERRITORY
TIGER

FORGET UFOs and the Yowie – the biggest Territory mystery of all could be the Territory Tiger.

This grainy still was taken from footage filmed by Territory resident Jan Donovan.

Author Rebecca Lang, who has spent five years compiling reports of sightings and collecting photos for a new book, said this large sandy-coloured cat was a "considerable size".

INSIDE › OUR FULL REPORT: P2

THE BEAUTIFUL GIRLS DISCOVERY THIS FRIDAY

NORTHERN TERRITORY NEWS

Phone: 89449900 Classifieds: 8944 9999 www.ntnews.com.au
Friday, June 27, 2008
$1.20* (Country freight) Incl. GST
20 cents extra

UFOs invade NT town

'The ground ... was shaking, so we ran inside'

By TASH HENNIG

A SMALL Territory community is still reeling with shock after four UFOs descended on their Outback homes.

Families spent hours in fear as what appeared to be three spaceships hovered in the distance with another just metres above their houses.

The drama at Marlinja, population 112 and 730km south of Darwin, began at 8pm on Sunday.

Resident Janie Dixon said it started as an "ordinary" night.

"The kids were on the

Continued Page 2

WAS IT LIKE THIS?: A scene from Steven Spielberg's classic movie, **Close Encounters of the Third Kind**

❛ The light in the house became so bright, it was like we were in a stadium ❜

❛ The kids at the basketball courts ran — two stood there looking to the sky ❜

❛ It came closer, circled around the courts and so close above our house ❜

❛ Then we saw three red lights and the sound kept on getting louder ❜

NT News

YOUR VOICE IN THE TERRITORY

Monday, May 12, 2014   ntnews.com.au $1.20 Country freight 20 cents extra* Incl GST

ALIENS' CIRCLE WORK

UFO blamed for bizarre Outback 'crop circle'

Picture: RAY AYLETT

Lawrie Fuchs studies a mysterious circle that has appeared in rough ground on remote Muckaty Station

'There's no other explanation' >> P2

MUM'S DAY FUN RUN

WE'VE GOT ALL YOUR PHOTOS >> P5

THE BARRA NATIONALS

FINAL RESULTS AND FULL PIC COVERAGE >> P9

V1 - NTNE01Z01MA

WHEN ANIMALS GO WILD

TERRITORIANS love animals.

We don't mean love them as in 'I love cats . . . but can't eat a whole one!' No, we love having them around. We love sharing our personal space with them.

We have crocs in our pools, snakes in our loos, dogs in our knicker drawers, buffaloes in our spas, and killer peacocks in our worst nightmares.

And our animals are smart. Really smart. Smarter than everyone else's animals. Well, except for the talking cat. He only has a vocabulary of seven words. And two of those are swear words.

Which, when you think of it, is probably about the same swear-word ratio as you'd find in your average Territorian's vocabulary. So #$%@ it! He *is* smart after all!

OUR DOG ATE MY G-STRING

By REBEKAH CAVANAGH

A TERRITORY dog's knickers fetish almost cost him his life when he swallowed his owner's G-string over the Easter long weekend.

Vets said that elastic on the size 10, lacy, black G-string became wrapped around the intestines of Baxter, *(pictured on the operating table)* a two-year-old cavalier king charles spaniel.

Baxter's owner, who was too embarrassed to be named, said she rushed her tiny pooch to the University Avenue

Continued Page 2

Picture: BRAD FLEET

EXPLOSIVE EXCLUSIVE Govt agrees to fireworks ban

By BEN LANGFORD

PRIVATE fireworks will be banned on Mindil Beach this Territory Day after a bombshell backflip by the NT Government.

Attorney-General Delia Lawrie has said the Government will now support Darwin City Council's plans to restrict public fireworks on the iconic beach. The change of policy has not been made public but is revealed in a letter to the council from Ms Lawrie.

"The Northern Territory Government is willing to work with the DCC to restrict fireworks on Mindil Beach to a DCC organised public display or permit displays only," Ms Lawrie wrote.

"The Northern Territory Government ... will support a restriction on private fireworks used on Mindil Beach, but not on other council controlled land."

The ban will mean the official display of fireworks, fired from barges in the water, may be the only crackers allowed at Mindil on July 1.

Darwin City Council has been considering a permit system after scenes of mayhem at the beach last Territory Day. Chief Minister Paul Henderson last year vowed to oppose the council's ban.

"If it means putting legislation through Territory Parliament to ensure that Darwin City Council cannot tie up Territorians in red tape one night of the year where thousands of people enjoy cracker night, that's what we'll do," he said in July.

The issue came to a head last year when council officers at Mindil were turned on by hoons after crackers were let off into the crowd.

The dispute saw the Government and the council engage in a war of

Continued Page 3

NORTHERN TERRITORY NEWS

Still only

Phone: 8944 9900 Classifieds: 8944 9999 www.ntnews.com.au   Saturday, September 5, 2009 $1.60* (Country freight 50 cents extra) Incl. GST

GIANT SNAKE IN LOO

'It would certainly give anyone a fright - it'd scare the pants off you. Well, you've probably already got you're pants off, but it'd scare you if you looked down and saw it'

SNAKE 3.5 metres

ERIK 1.7 metres

TOILET .9 metre

READ THE AMAZING STORY, MORE PICTURES: P2

TRI NATIONS 2NITE K.O SPORTS BAR @KITTYS

SUNDAY Territorian

September 25, 2011 | $1.30 Country freight 20c extra. Includes GST

MUTANT 5-LEGGED TOADZILLA

DETAILS ▶ P7

BOY, 11, CHARGED OVER SCHOOL FIGHT

FULL STORY ≫P6

GREAT WEEKEND READING ▷

Escape | body+soul | Taste | Donna Hay | Sunday

UFC 135 10.30AM KO'S

NT ★ News

YOUR VOICE IN THE TERRITORY

Tuesday, April 8, 2014   ntnews.com.au $1.20 Country freight 20 cents extra Incl GST

GORGEOUS GEORGE STEALS THE SHOW

REPORT »P15

RAPID CREEK LAND 'VANDALISM'

STORY »P5

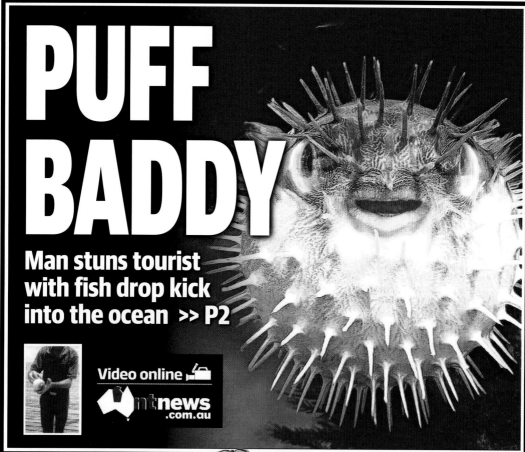

PUFF BADDY

Man stuns tourist with fish drop kick into the ocean »> P2

Video online nt**news** .com.au

Bowser budget blowout

TERRITORIANS spend more on transport than food, according to the latest cost of living report.

It is the only jurisdiction in the nation where transport has a bigger impact on budgets than food.

Stuart Park mother Tabitha Brett, *pictured left* with daughter,

Isabella Webster, spends more on fuel than groceries, filling up at least twice a week. The report revealed transport costs were driven by the increasing price of fuel, which has jumped 127 per cent in Darwin over the past 15 years.
Full story: Page 3

Despair at needless death

A MAN killed in a "fireball" when a pensioner crashed into his car could still be alive if plans for a panel to take medically unfit drivers off the road weren't abandoned in 2007, a court has been told.

Benjamin Wilton would have turned 31 today but instead his

mum, brother and fiancee are listening to the inquest into his "horrific" death before the NT Coroner.

Robert Frank Spencer, now aged 69, was acquitted of criminal charges on grounds of mental impairment.
Full story: Page 7

NEW DOCUMENTS SHED LIGHT ON UFO MYSTERY ⟩ P16

V1 - NTNE01Z01MA

NORTHERN TERRITORY NEWS

56 PAGES

Phone: 8944 9900 Classifieds: 8944 9999 www.ntnews.com.au

Friday, May 14, 2010

$1.20* (Country freight 20 cents extra) Incl. GST

Horny roo stalks NT women

By JASMIN AFIANOS

A BRAWNY kangaroo that has been seeking love of late has focussed his lust on the women of a Territory town.

The well-endowed macropod has been hanging around the Honeymoon Ranges in Tennant Creek recently, making every effort to woo a woman.

One resident who walks along the bike track to the Mary Ann Dam regularly said she realised she was being followed early one morning.

"I turned around and saw this big kangaroo behind me, so I hastened my steps," she said.

"It seemed a bit odd, but I continued walking and didn't think much about it.

"Then on the return walk he was there waiting for me," she said.

"With his male pride on full alert, he started circling me.

"There was no doubt about what he wanted, the randy old thing.

"It was a huge kangaroo and quite intimidating.

"I yelled at him to go

Continued Page 2

Inpex delayed again but Govt sure it's still coming

By NICK CALACOURAS

TERRITORIANS will have to wait even longer for the final investment decision from Inpex — with the date of completion pushed back beyond 2015.

Inpex director Masahiro Murayama said in Tokyo that the company would not make a decision this year or meet its 2015 start of operations deadline. He did not provide a reason for the delay.

Inpex spokesman Sean Kildare said last night the company's president Naoki Kuroda would be giving a project update to investors this afternoon in Tokyo.

But Chief Minister Paul Henderson said he had been assured the project was still coming.

Mr Henderson said he had been given a confidential briefing by the Japanese energy giant — but he could not disclose what he was told.

"What I can say is I get regular updates, and I have been assured very recently that this project will come to Darwin," he said.

Many Territorians were disappointed to learn last month that the Greater Sunrise gas project would not come to Darwin — and would be processed on an experimental offshore facility.

This new technology could hurt the Territory's chances for future gas projects.

But Mr Henderson said this would not happen to the Inpex project.

"For some fields, like Inpex, are too big and it would be impossible to develop with a floating platform," he

Continued Page 4

NT ◆ News

YOUR VOICE IN THE TERRITORY

Monday, February 17, 2014   ntnews.com.au $1.20 Country freight 20 cents extra Incl GST

SNAKE EYES

Who won this incredible stare-off? »P5

Picture: JESSIE TEARLE

LAW AND DISORDER

MORE COMPLAINTS AGAINST NT POLICE THAN ANY OTHER FORCE

PAGE 5

WOMAN KILLED, 3 SERIOUSLY INJURED IN HORROR HEAD-ON

FULL REPORT »P2

NT News

YOUR VOICE IN THE TERRITORY

Monday, April 2, 2012 ntnews.com.au $1.20 Country freight 20 cents extra Incl GST

JUST FOOTY
NEW 8-PAGE LIFTOUT INSIDE
☐ AFL and NRL match wraps ☐ Stats ☐ Scoreboards ☐ Ladders

TOADALLY LAZY
NT's mutant supertoads croak in fitness tests against interstate rivals

STORY ⟩ P2

SEX DRIVE

You won't believe what you'll see on the side of the Stuart Highway **REVEALED** ⟩⟩PAGE 3

GET YOUR PAPER HOME DELIVERED CALL 8944 9903

NT✦News

YOUR VOICE IN THE TERRITORY

Thursday, December 5, 2013   ntnews.com.au $1.20 Country freight 30 cents extra Incl GST

AUSSIES FIRE UP FOR ADELAIDE TEST
»SPORT

OUR TRIBUTE TO RETURNED SOLDIERS
SPECIAL REPORT »P7

Picture: ELISE DERWIN

THEY STOLE MY DOG WHILE I WAS ON THE BOG

Council cops a spray from jogger on the runs

EXPOOSIVE ▸ P2

YOUR VOICE IN THE TERRITORY

NT News

Thursday, July 5, 2012   ntnews.com.au $1.20 Country freight 30 cents extra   Inc GST

MAN "BASHED TO DEATH WITH HAMMER"

REPORT » P3

MAROONS HOME IN THRILLER

STORY, PICS » P10-11, SPORT

IT'S A SINGING DOG

FREDDIE BARK-URY

Picture: JUSTIN SANSON

FIND OUT WHY THIS TERRITORY BITCH IS QUEEN » P8

WIN $$$$ WITH KARAOKE AT THE BEACHFRONT 9PM 2NITE

NORTHERN TERRITORY NEWS

Phone 8944 9900   CLASSIFIEDS: 8944 9999   **DARWIN: Saturday, June 25, 2005** $1.50* (Country Freight / 30 cents extra) Incl. GST

Don't be fooled by his beauty. Meet the bird from hell ...

Peacock terrorises van park

One tough bird ... the peacock struts through the caravan park yesterday; and (above) victim Stefan Poeltl's battle scars. Pictures: PETER BENNETT

By REBEKAH CAVANAGH

A feral peacock has gone on the rampage at a Territory caravan park, attacking guests and cars.

The bird has been roaming the Shady Glen park in Winnellie, Darwin, for 18 months.

It started scratching cars — and then graduated to clawing and

Continued: Page 2

NORTHERN TERRITORY NEWS

Phone: 8944 9900 CLASSIFIEDS: 8944 9999   DARWIN: Thursday,   February 16, 2006 $1.10¹ (Country Freight) 20 cents extra Incl. GST

NO MERCY
Final Bali three jailed for life **P14**

YOUR LATEST HEALTH & FITNESS TIPS

health & fitness

● TAKE IT
● AWAY

SUPER TOAD

■ **Bigger**
■ **Stronger**
■ **Faster**

Invaders evolving rapidly

By KAREN MICHELMORE

IT HAS invaded the Territory and now the hated cane toad is evolving — growing faster, longer legs as it rampages through the Top End.

Researchers have been studying the toxic pests in the NT, clocking them hopping up to 2km in a single night, or more than 50km a year — five times quicker than their predecessors travelled in the 1940s to 1960s.

Continued Page 5

NT★News

YOUR VOICE IN THE TERRITORY

Friday, November 30, 2012   ntnews.com.au $1.20 Country freight 20 cents extra Incl GST

2012 BRAND OF THE YEAR

PUNTER'S LAST STAND
DETAILS ≫SPORT

WHO'S OFF THE LIST
150 MOST POWERFUL ≫P18, 19

Picture: ELISE DERWIN

FROG STRUCK DOWN BY LIGHTNING

... and a few humans were nearly hit too ≫P2

TERRITORY SCHOOL BANS CHRISTMAS CARDS ⟩ PAGE 3

NORTHERN TERRITORY NEWS

Still only

Phone: 8944 9900 **Classifieds:** 8944 9999 www.ntnews.com.au

Saturday, August 29, 2009

$1.60* (Country freight 30 cents extra) **Incl. GST**

FUR DINKUM!

It's a talking cat

Meow do you do?

STORY >P9

WE HEARD HIM SPEAK!

... and he's a Territorian – he swears!

Mischief's vocabulary

- Mum • No • Now
- • What • F**k
- • Prick • Why

NT News

YOUR VOICE IN THE TERRITORY

Friday, August 13, 2010   ntnews.com.au $1.20 Country freight 30cents extra Incl GST

ASK BOSSY
How can I get my girlfriend to stop stripping? **»P23**

Win a Kakadu flight and cruise
Prize value $1000 **»P37**

This dog thinks he's a chicken
INSIDE ► MURRAY'S STORY: P9

Picture: NICK WELSH

MAN BASHED BY PRAWN

By NADJA HAINKE

A MAN was slammed in the face with a block of prawns when he caught an intruder going through his fridge.

The 37-year-old man was left with injuries to his left hand, eye and forehead.

He told police: "It was like getting hit in the face with a rock."

◄ Continued Page 2

LINGERIE MODEL COMP DISCOVERY TOMORROW

NT●News

YOUR VOICE IN THE TERRITORY

Thursday, September 6, 2012   ntnews.com.au $1.20 Country freight 20cents extra Incl GST

News Destination PANPA AWARDS **2011** Of The Year

DRUG SQUAD COP 'CAUGHT ON CAMERA'

COURT REPORT »**P3**

OUR HEROES COME HOME

STORY »**P15**

BATHING IN THE BUFF

INSIDE
READ THE FULL STORY »**P2**

Couple shocked to find wild beast frolicking... in their spa

MISS HONEY POT 2012 FINALS – 2NITE

NT News

YOUR VOICE IN THE TERRITORY

Monday, January 13, 2014 · ntnews.com.au · $1.20 Country freight 30 cents extra Incl GST

BLESSING OF THE WATERS
GOOD YEAR AHEAD ≫P3

THIEF HIDES CASK IN PANTS
PLEASED TO SEE YOU ≫P2

RUFF JUSTICE

- **DOG COPS FINE FOR NOT WEARING SEATBELT**
- **OWNER BARKING MAD**

FULL STORY P4

Picture: MICHAEL FRANCHI

GIRLS GONE WILD

- **ARRESTS MADE WHEN TEENS BRAWL IN STREET AFTER PARTY**
- **ANGRY MOB OF KIDS THROWS BOTTLES AT POLICE** REPORT ≫ P2

NT★News

YOUR VOICE IN THE TERRITORY

Wednesday, April 16, 2014   ntnews.com.au   **$1.20** Country freight 20 cents extra **Incl GST**

Don't risk your life

HONK IF YOU'RE HORNY

FULL STORY »P2

BLACK★LIST

✗ **Report reveals litany of errors caused 12-hour blackout**

✗ **PWC entrenched in culture of "union cronyism", says Tollner**

REPORT »P2

V1 - NTNE01Z01MA

NT News

YOUR VOICE IN THE TERRITORY

Wednesday, February 26, 2014   ntnews.com.au $1.20 Country freight 30 cents extra Incl GST

CROC ESCAPES JAIL
STORY ≫ P5

BEST AND WORST OF DARWIN LIFE
REVEALED ≫ P8

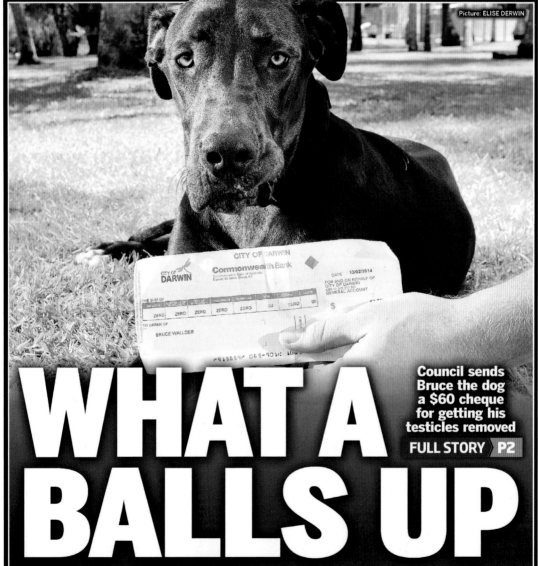

Picture: ELISE DERWIN

WHAT A BALLS UP

Council sends Bruce the dog a $60 cheque for getting his testicles removed

FULL STORY ⟩ P2

GILES SIGNS NEW TRADE AGREEMENT WITH VIETNAM ⟩ **BUSINESS WEEK STARTS P23**

YOUR VOICE IN THE TERRITORY

NT News

Monday, December 23, 2013   ntnews.com.au $1.20 Country freight 50 cents extra* incl GST

TERRITORY CROCS ARE GETTING SMARTER

STORY >>P11

CELEBRATING OUR YEAR 12 GRADUATES

16 PAGE LIFTOUT INSIDE TODAY

NTCET

CELEBRATING OUR YEAR 12 GRADUATES

BEACHED AS, BRO

SANDY SOUTHERNER TAKES A DRIVE ON THE WILD SIDE

TXN EQUIPPED

FISH01

FULL STORY ▶ P5

HORNY SNAKE SURPRISE

WOMAN SHOCKED BY UNEXPECTED BEDMATE

FIND OUT MORE >>P2

CASUARINA SQUARE OPEN LATE UNTIL 9PM

NT News

Monday, March 18, 2013   ntnews.com.au $1.20 Country freight 20cents extra   Incl GST

GRAPES OF WRATH
FRUITY FALL COST $6000 »P2

ALL THE ACTION FROM THE TIWI GRAND FINAL
PAGES 8, 9, SPORT

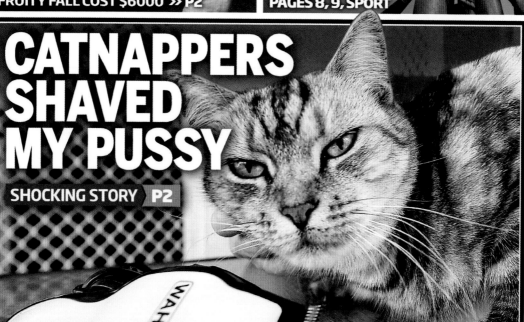

CATNAPPERS SHAVED MY PUSSY

SHOCKING STORY **P2**

Picture: PATRINA MALONE

HOT TO TROT

INSIDE

FULL REPORT »P3

• MAN THROWS PETROL ON BBQ THAT 'WASN'T HOT ENOUGH' • SHOES GO UP IN FLAMES

VISIT OUR NEW MOBILE SITE M.NTNEWS.COM.AU TODAY

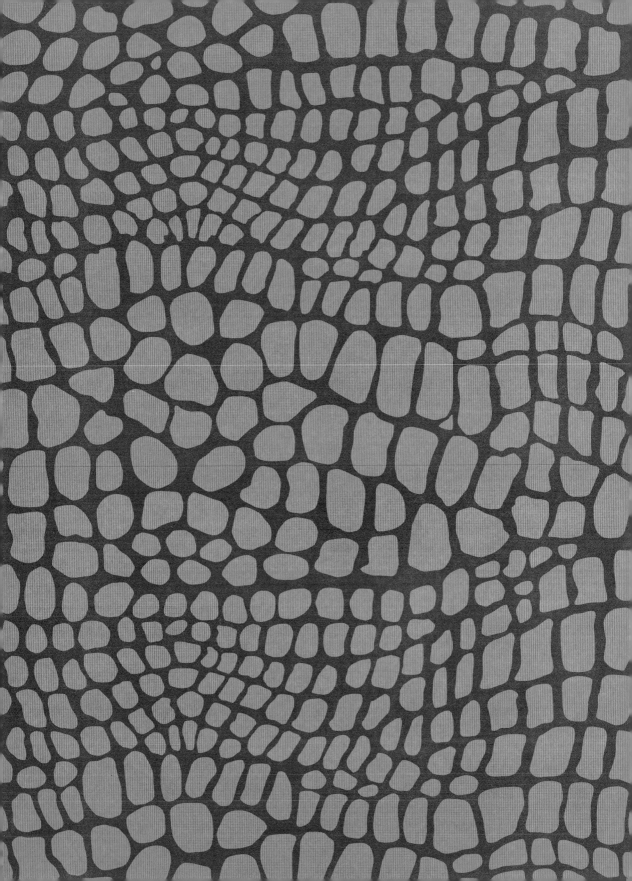

THE NAKED
TRUTH

DID we tell you that it's hot in the Territory? No? OK, well, it's hot in the Territory. Damn hot! All the time.

That probably explains why some Territorians drink a lot. To replace fluids . . . and stuff. And why some of them believe that clothing often should be optional. To keep cool in the heat . . . and stuff.

Sometimes, when both of these activities take place at the same time, things can go a tad awry.

Like the time when the tipsy pub robber thought it would be a good idea to completely disrobe in front of the CCTV cameras while on a stealing spree. But many other locals don't need to drink to realise it's a good thing to get naked. Thank goodness.

Some of our greatest Territorians have shown the right stuff while in the buff. Like the time when a heroic hottie put out a hotel fire while topless, prompting this fine witness description: 'Once she had the blaze under control, she then got her bikini situation under control.'

As we like to say at the *NT News*, 'No nudes is not good news.'

107

NORTHERN TERRITORY NEWS

Still only

Phone: 89449900 Classifieds: 8944 9999 www.ntnews.com.au   **Wednesday, June 17, 2009** $1.20* (Country freight 20 cents extra) Incl. GST

Man stabbed eight times in 'road rage' attack

SHOCKING REPORT »3

MUNDINE MOCKS GREEN OVER NT REMATCH IDEA »47

Kelly gang ready to rumble

IT'S V8 TIME »46

Saltie food in the nude

CROC A-TACK-LE: Now that's something you don't see every day

No tops, no jocks, mind the crocs!

By ALYSSA BETTS

TAKE a squiz at this disrobed duo capering about on top of what appears to be a Territory croc trap.

Risking life, limb and a couple of other bits, the dakless duo are clambering on top of a cage filled with bait meant to entice man-eating beasts. The photo was sent to the *Northern Territory News* by SMS with the suggested caption:

Continued Page 2

"NO MORE..." STRONG FAMILY AWARD PH 8941 9111

NT News

YOUR VOICE IN THE TERRITORY

Monday, November 26, 2012 ntnews.com.au $1.20 *(recommended)* incl GST

2012 BRAND OF THE YEAR

FLASH MORON

Car salesman exposes himself at popular tourist spot during "animalistic" rampage on Anzac Day

READ THE FULL STORY »PAGE 4

TERRITORIANS TURN BACK ON PARADISE
BILL BUSTERS »P3

FOOTY PLAYER STUNG BY DEADLY JELLYFISH
REVEALED »P9

NORTHERN TERRITORY NEWS

Phone 8944 9900   CLASSIFIEDS: 8944 9999   **DARWIN: Friday, April 19, 2002** $1.00* (Country Freight 20 cents extra) Incl. GST

HUMAN NATURE AMPHITHEATRE OPENS AGAIN
PAGE 15

SCHOOLS BRING BACK THREE Rs
PAGE 3

Nudists want bigger beach

It's one of Darwin's tourist attractions

Mr Gray yesterday ... rangers are booking nudists walking to the beach's original boundary. Picture: DANI GAWLIK

By SUELLEN HINDE

Darwin nudist Lindsay Gray wants Casuarina's "free" beach extended by 500 metres.

Mr Gray says the beach is used by more regulars than any other in Darwin "except maybe for dog walkers".

"The beach is a tourist attraction; you often come across Americans and Europeans taking a stroll," he said.

He claimed the move would help prevent instances of Parks and Wildlife Commission rangers booking nudists walking to the beach's original boundary.

Mr Gray believes the free beach should be returned to the original area designated for nudity in 1976 — from the Casuarina car park to Sandfly Creek.

He has approached the commission to consider his request through its draft plan of management for Casuarina Coastal Reserve.

The commission is seeking public input to form a final plan of management for the area and is inviting public submissions.

Continued, Page 2

Yunupingu not guilty of murder: P3

NORTHERN TERRITORY NEWS

Phone: 8944 9900 Classifieds: 8944 9999 www.ntnews.com.au **Thursday, January 15, 2009** $1.20* (Country freight 20 cents extra) Incl. GST

CHARGED OVER A 1 CENT BILL

STORY » PAGE 3

Start of something big
NT FOOTY HISTORY

REPORT, PICTURES » SPORT

FAST FOOD IN THE NUDE

... but where does this customer stash the cash?

By NADJA HAINKE

A MAN was served hot chips at a Territory eatery wearing nothing but his birthday suit.

The late night reveller stripped bare before putting in his order at the Darwin City 24-Eatery on Smith St early on Monday. A witness said the naked man walked into the shop to order two buckets of chips with gravy.

And the female attendant was reportedly only too happy to serve the nude customer.

Steven Bastick, 23, watched the naked act when he walked past the eatery.

He said he "bumped into" two men standing in front of the shop. "I was just walking

Continued Page 2

FROM BAGS TO RICHES

THEY started out penniless, barefoot and wearing garbage bags.
Four months later, Gareth Owen, Anne Race and Phil Carr have travelled more than 10,000km and raised $9000 for charity.
> **FULL STORY: P3**
Picture: CHLOE ERLICH

NT☘News

YOUR VOICE IN THE TERRITORY

PANPA AWARDS News Destination Of The Year 2011

Thursday, September 29, 2011   ntnews.com.au $1.20 Country freight 20 cents extra Incl GST

EXCLUSIVE

EYEFUL TOWER

CROWDS FLOCK TO SEE SEX IN THE CITY

Oh, did we mention we have video?

DETAILS ≫P2

COP DIVES IN RIVER TO RESCUE WOMAN AS CROCS CIRCLE ≫P3

NT News

YOUR VOICE IN THE TERRITORY

Monday, May 20, 2013   ntnews.com.au $1.20 Country Enquire 20cents extra Incl GST

WIN TICKETS TO THE BARUNGA FESTIVAL

FIND OUT HOW >> P6

ALL THE AFL AND NRL SCORES AND STATS

JUST FOOTY >> INSIDE

DUMB AND BUMMER

A woman crashed her car after being distracted by her passenger who was trying to "moon" a semi-trailer as they overtook it on the Stuart Highway   **MEAGAN DILLON REPORTS** **P2**

THRILLS AND SPILLS AT NOONAMAH

RODEO ACTION >> P7

IS THIS THE END FOR HOLDEN?

REPORT >> P3

NORTHERN TERRITORY **NEWS**

Phone: 8944 9900   Classifieds: 8944 9999   www.ntnews.com.au   **Tuesday, May 11, 2010** $1.20* (Country freight 20 cents extra) Incl. GST

WIN AFL TICKETS

Details >> P36

HOT STUFF: Heroic accidental exhibitionist, Tash Bennett (left), with her sister Liz. Tash saved an apartment building from going up in flames but forgot she was topless at the time

Topless heroine puts out hotel fire

'Once she had the blaze under control she got her bikini top under control'

By **NICK CALACOURAS**

A WOMAN put the safety of her neighbours over her own modesty when she saved an apartment building from going up in flames — while topless.

One witness, Johnny McCoy said the heroic hottie had a full audience of the block's residents while she battled the blaze.

"For the record, she was smoking hot herself, but

Continued Page 2

HAPPY MOTHER'S DAY:
DEATH ADDER GIVES BIRTH TO 30 BUBS > P3

AUSTRALIAN SPRINTCAR TITLE 27-29 MAY

NT News

YOUR VOICE IN THE TERRITORY

Wednesday, October 2, 2013 · ntnews.com.au · $1.20 Country freight 20 cents extra · Incl GST

MIKE SHEAHAN'S AFL TOP 50
PART 1 >> P40

WIN ONE OF 20 FAMILY PASSES TO PLANES
DETAILS >> P20

JAMIE GETS DOWN TO BUSINESS
STORY >> P7

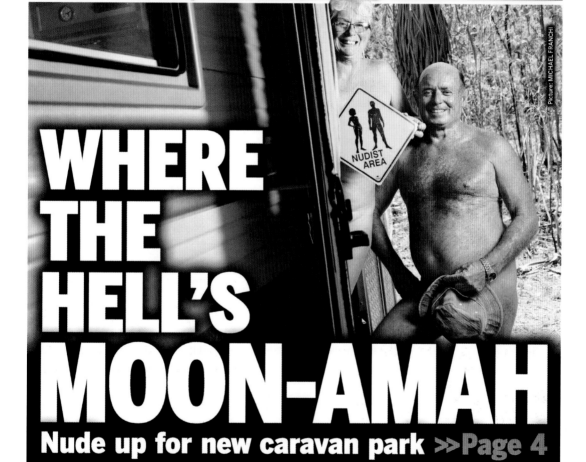

Picture: MICHAEL FRANCHI

NUDIST AREA

WHERE THE HELL'S MOON-AMAH

Nude up for new caravan park >> Page 4

NT News

YOUR VOICE IN THE TERRITORY

Tuesday, July 30, 2013   ntnews.com.au $1.20 Country freight 50cents extra Incl GST

2012 BRAND OF THE YEAR

DISCOUNT FUEL DOCKETS MAY BE SCRAPPED
FIND OUT WHY ≫ P5

THE 100 BEST AUSSIE TV CHARACTERS
WHO IS YOUR FAVOURITE? ≫ P15-17

WAX ON, RACKS OFF
BUBBLE TROUBLE AS COPS STOP TOPLESS CAR CLEANERS: P2

'HE'S BEEN THROUGH A LIVING HELL'

SON REVEALS TRUE STORY BEHIND DAD'S KILLER RAMPAGE

EXCLUSIVE ⟩ P4

NT News

YOUR VOICE IN THE TERRITORY

Thursday, April 4, 2013   ntnews.com.au $1.20 Country freight 20 cents extra Incl GST

SEARCH CALLED OFF AFTER PLANE CRASH

TRIBUTES ≫P3

NT GOVT FLAGS RETURN OF OPEN SPEED LIMITS

REPORT ≫P5

SURF'S UP, NUDE

DAREDEVIL TACKLES CROCS AND FLOOD FOR GROG ≫P2

ACKNOWLEDGMENTS

To all the Territorians, Southerners and overseas tourists who through their tales have contributed to making the *NT News* one of the world's most-loved papers, we salute you. Thanks also to the editors, journos and snappers past and present who tell their stories so eloquently each day. And a special shout out to our mate Brutus the croc, love ya work.

Keep up with the latest from *NT News*
www.ntnews.com.au
facebook: The NT News
twitter: @TheNTNews

If you would like to find out more about Hachette Australia, upcoming events and new releases you can visit our website or follow us on Twitter.

www.hachette.com.au
www.twitter.com/HachetteAus